20/20

20/20

A TOTAL GUIDE TO
Improving Your Vision
AND
Preventing Eye Disease

By Mitchell H. Friedlaender, M.D.,
Division of Ophthalmology,
Scripps Clinic and Research Foundation,
and Stef Donev

Rodale Press, Emmaus, Pennsylvania

Notice

This book is intended as a reference volume only, not as a medical guide or manual for self-treatment. If you suspect that you have a medical problem, please seek competent medical care. The information here is designed to help you make informed choices about your health. It is not intended as a substitute for any treatment prescribed by your doctor.

Cover and interior design: *Lisa Farkas*

Illustrations: *Jean Gardner*

Copy Editor: *Candace Levy*

Indexer: *Kathleen D. Bagioni*

If you have any questions or comments concerning this book, please write:
Rodale Press
Book Reader Service
33 East Minor Street
Emmaus, PA 18098

Library of Congress Cataloging-in-Publication Data

Friedlaender, Mitchell H.
    20/20: a total guide to improving your vision and preventing eye disease /
by Mitchell H. Friedlaender and Stef Donev.
        p.   cm.
    Includes index.
    ISBN 0–87857–930–3 hardcover
    1. Vision—Popular works. 2. Eyes—Care and hygiene. 3. Eyes—Diseases and defects—Popular works. I. Donev, Stef. II. Title. III. Title: Twenty/twenty.
RE51.F75   1990
617.7—dc20   90–9088
                                                                      CIP

Distributed in the book trade by St. Martin's Press

2 4 6 8 10 9 7 5 4 3 1 hardcover

To our wives, Mary and Debbie. And to Agnes.
They helped in more ways than we would care
to admit.

CONTENTS

ACKNOWLEDGMENTS

The authors would like to gratefully acknowledge the assistance and cooperation of the following people and organizations. They made the researching and writing of this book much, much simpler.

American Academy of Ophthalmology

American Optometric Association

National Society to Prevent Blindness, Inc.

Research to Prevent Blindness

Thomas P. Rogers, O.D.

John Feltman

I

INTRODUCTION

While bookstores are filled with volumes that tell us what to eat, when and how to exercise, and how to take care of our backs and our knees, we find a huge void when we look under the subject of eyes.

Could it be that people are not that interested in their vision? Or is the fear of losing the use of our eyes—going blind—too frightening to think about?

Is the universal "If I don't think about it, it can't happen to me" assumption at work here? It's hard to be sure.

When an eye doctor encounters a health-conscious person, however, you can be sure the conversation will eventually—and often quickly—turn to the topic of eyes and eye care.

Now, in all fairness, our eyes are pretty good at taking care of themselves. Nature has endowed us with mechanisms that help protect our eyes from flying objects, dust particles, inconsiderate birds, and snowball fights.

The eyes produce tears that constantly moisten the surface of the eye and wash away debris, while the blinking eyelids act like windshield wipers, sweeping germs and cinders into the corners of the eye, pushing them away from the clear optical tissues through which we see.

But as with any other system in the body, things can and sometimes do go haywire, or just plain wear out. That's when the eyes may have to be fixed.

And just as we can tune a car for better performance, there are things we can do to protect our eyes and make them function longer and smoother. But we should know how to spot trouble when it occurs. Sometimes we need to let nature take its course so the eye can heal itself, but we should also know when to call on professional healers—especially if we have a family history of diseases such as glaucoma or diabetes.

This book is designed to educate you about your eyes. It will tell you how the eye works and why it sometimes does not work. It will tell you when to see your eye doctor and when to stay home. It will answer the questions about eye problems you may have and problems that you and your loved ones may develop. It will answer questions about cataract surgery, lens implants, laser treatments, and much more.

We have tried to make *20/20* an open, honest discussion of eye problems and the eye care profession. We have tried to distinguish the scientific facts from the old wives' tales. And we have written about the new treatments that are being used now and those that may become available in the future.

The book deals with a multitude of topics. We hope to guide you through this maze of information and to prepare you to care for your eyes and make decisions about them. If we accomplish this, we will have done our job, helping you to enjoy the wonderful gift of sight for a lifetime.

█ CHAPTER 1

YOUR EYES
AN OWNER'S MANUAL

"On a Clear Day, You Can See Forever"

Song title (fiction)

From orbit, astronauts can see the Great Wall of China and the wakes of oceangoing ships.

Fact (and almost as impressive)

If you want a basic understanding of how your eyes work, get a camera. You can ignore the tripod, timer, flash attachment, bayonet lens mountings, motor drives, fancy case, and all the other extras, doodads, and add-ons. Just concentrate on the basic Kodak box camera that George Eastman introduced to the world in 1888. The famous box was built to hold two items: a lens and film. God supplied the sunlight, and you decided what to take a picture of.

Your eyes are a million or so times more complicated than that, but if you keep the camera analogy in your mind, you shouldn't have too much trouble following along as we look at the mechanics of vision.

The Lens System

Let's start out with the two external requirements for vision—light and something to look at. When light strikes an object, the light rays are reflected off that object and into your own biological camera. With the original Kodak, the "lens system" was just a piece of ground glass that focused the image on the film.

The same basic thing happens when the light strikes your eye. The image is focused on the retina, which functions like the film. But the human lens system it passes through is more than just a piece of ground glass.

First the light passes through the cornea, a clear lens that covers the front part of the eye in much the same way that a watch crystal covers the face of a watch.

Once through the cornea, the image enters a narrow space known as the anterior chamber. This space is filled with a liquid called the aqueous humor. Next the image passes through the pupil. While the pupil looks black, it is actually a hole in the center of the iris, the colored part of the eye. Once through the pupil, the image is actually "inside" the eye.

The image then passes through the crystalline lens, usually referred to simply as the lens, then on through the vitreous body, the jellylike substance your eyes are filled with.

"Just what do you mean by filled?" you might ask. Well, the average human eye weighs about 7 grams (about ¼ ounce). Of that, nearly 4 grams are vitreous.

After getting through the vitreous body, the image has traveled approximately an inch through your eyes and finally reaches its target, the retina.

The retina sits like a lining on the inside of the back part of the eye. It contains a million or so light-sensitive cells, called rods and cones. These are what actually "take" the pictures. And they take them constantly. All the time your eyes are open, they're clicking off more shots than a busload of tourists at the

Grand Canyon. Even when there isn't any light they're still taking pictures. They just happen to come out black—underexposed.

The light-sensitive rods and cones have long nerve endings that come together like the stems in a bouquet of flowers and form the optic nerve. As the optic nerves of the right eye and left eye travel through the skull, they merge and then separate again to form the right and left optic tracts.

The fibers of the right optic tract "see" the right half of the field of vision for both the right and the left eye. Similarly, the fibers of the left optic tract "see" the left half of the field of vision for both eyes. After a long, circuitous path through the brain, the fibers finally reach the occipital lobes in the very back of the brain. All the images that the optic nerves transmit to the occipital lobes are stored, sorted, and interpreted by the brain.

It's worth remembering that while your eyes take the pictures, it is the brain that actually interprets what you see. When you close your eyes and recall an image or picture out of the past, you are seeing it with your brain. People who have gone blind can still "see" images in their minds that they "photographed" through their eyes before they lost their vision.

Parts and Accessories

You have just completed the short course on how your eyes work. For more specific information, you'll have to keep on reading. We'll go into the various parts of the eye in more detail, and also look at some of the accessories.

Eyelids

To continue the comparison between your eyes and a camera, the eyelids function as combination lens covers and lens cleaners. Aside from any conscious winking or blinking you might do, the subconscious centers of the brain have your eyelids blink at regular intervals of five to ten times a minute to sweep away small foreign particles such as dust, dirt, or dandruff. Blinking also keeps the surface of the eye moist and smooth by coating it evenly with a thin layer of tears.

The lids also help protect the eyes from wind, dust, fingers, snowballs, coat hangers, and other hazards. A protective response known as the blink reflex kicks in whenever you sense danger to your eyes. They automatically close fast and tight at the first indication of a flying fist or the beam of a flashlight.

Conjunctiva

The conjunctiva is a thin, transparent, protective membrane that covers most of the front part of the eye. Similar to the lining inside your nose and mouth, it also lines the inner surface of the eyelid.

The little bumps at the inner corners of the eyes are special folds of conjunctiva that help direct the flow of tears into ducts located at the inner margins of the eyelids. When the conjunctiva is irritated by rubbing, infection, contact lenses, smoke, or dust and dirt, its blood vessels dilate (widen) and the eye appears red or bloodshot. Although bloodshot eyes might not look very nice, in some respects they are good for you. Because the blood vessels are enlarged, more blood can circulate through them, carrying away toxic substances and bringing additional oxygen and white blood cells to the eye to fight off infection.

Not getting enough sleep also can make your eyes bloodshot. One reason for redness is that you tend to rub your eyes when you're tired. Another is that your eyes are probably drier than they should be because they've been open too long. Your eyes get a great deal of their necessary moisture while you're sleeping.

Sclera

Somehow it's doubtful that the phrase "don't fire until you see the sclera!" would have made it into the history books. But since a wise, but worried, soldier named Israel Putnam warned his comrades back in 1775 not to fire until they saw "the whites of their eyes," the exhortation has been preserved by history books, movies, sergeants, and even T-shirts.

The sclera lies beneath the conjunctiva and covers the eye the way horsehide covers a baseball. The only parts of the eye unprotected by the tough, rigid material is the cornea—where light enters the eye—and the hole in the back of the eye where the optic nerves exit the eye to carry the images to the brain. Thanks to its rigidity, the sclera helps the eye maintain its shape and also serves to protect the eye's more delicate inner workings from unfriendly flying objects like footballs or Frisbees.

Cornea

The cornea is the transparent lens that covers the front of the eye. The eye's most optically powerful lens, the cornea helps focus images on the retina.

Although it is firm, it consists mainly of water and protein and is one of your body's few living tissues that contain no nourishing blood vessels. Instead, it receives nourishment from nearby blood vessels in the conjunctiva and sclera and from tears and the aqueous humor. It gets its oxygen directly from the air.

There are two major advantages to the cornea's not having any blood vessels. First, since the cornea can't become bloodshot, it remains clear and easy to see through. Second, because cells in our blood are responsible for "rejecting" transplanted organs, the lack of blood vessels in the cornea makes it easier for the eye to "accept" a cornea transplant.

Iris

Blue-tinted sunglasses will change the colors that you see when you look through them, but blue eyes won't. The color of your iris does not really affect the quality of your vision. Eye color is largely a matter of inheritance, and all the color does is indicate how much pigment the iris contains.

People with blue eyes have relatively little pigment in the

iris, brown-eyed people have a lot of pigment, and people with green eyes are somewhere in the middle.

Pupil

Even though it may look like a black dot, the pupil is actually a hole in the center of the iris that lets the light enter the eye. But this is not your ordinary hole.

If you enter a dark room, the pupil enlarges, or dilates, like the diaphragm of a camera. If you go out into the bright sunlight, the pupil constricts, or becomes smaller. This pupillary reflex protects the eye against the entry of too much light.

See for yourself. Stand in front of a mirror and shine a light into just one eye. Then look at both eyes in the mirror and compare.

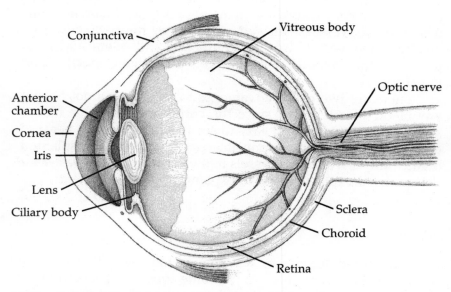

This cross section of the eye shows its similarities to a camera. Images that enter the eye are focused by the cornea and the lens, and then projected onto the retina, which acts as the film in the camera. The retina converts the image into electrical impulses that are carried to the brain through the optic nerve.

Light is not the only thing that a pupil responds to, however. When you see something that you like—especially if it's something that you *really* like—your pupil can get an extra 45 percent bigger, no matter how much or how little light there is.

Your eye doctor may shine a flashlight into each of your eyes to make sure the pupils are the same size and that they constrict with light. Because this reflex is controlled by nerves that extend from the back of the eyes to the back of the brain, unequal pupil size could be a sign of a stroke, brain tumor, concussion, or neurologic infection.

Choroid and Ciliary Body

Both the choroid and the ciliary body are pigmented tissues connected to the iris. They can be seen only through special examining equipment.

The ciliary body produces the watery fluid, known as the aqueous humor, that circulates throughout the eye. It supplies nutrition for the inside of the eye and also provides the pressure that keeps the eye in its normal shape.

Think of the eye in terms of a water balloon. When too much of the fluid is produced, or when it cannot drain out of the eye, you can develop a high–eye-pressure condition known as glaucoma, which will be discussed in more detail in chapter 9.

The choroid is sandwiched between the sclera and the retina and provides nutrition to the retina through its many tiny blood vessels. It absorbs energy from the photochemical processes that take place within the retina itself. Occasionally the choroid and other pigmented tissues within the eye can become inflamed, leading to a severe visual problem known as uveitis, which will also be discussed later.

Lens or Crystalline Lens

Usually referred to simply as the lens, the crystalline lens is located just behind the pupil, where it is suspended from the ciliary body by tiny fibers. It is enclosed in an elastic capsule that can be stretched to make the lens thicker or thinner.

As the lens thickens, it adds power to the eye and allows us to focus on close objects, such as the small print in a telephone book. This additional focusing power is called accommodation. But the flexibility that makes this accommodation possible diminishes as age increases. So by the time you're in your early forties, you'll probably need reading glasses or bifocals.

Vitreous

The vitreous is the clear, jellylike substance that fills the large cavity in the back two-thirds of the eye. It provides the eye with support and nutrition, but it can also cause problems.

Occasionally, bits of debris from the vitreous float around inside the eye. These "floaters" appear as spots before your eyes and are one of the most common visual complaints. A much more serious problem occurs when strands of the sticky, chewing-gum-like elastic vitreous stick to the retina. If a vitreous strand contracts, it can rip the delicate retina, leaving a hole or tear. This can possibly lead to a detached retina, a vision-robbing condition that will be covered in chapter 11.

Retina

Lying on the inner surface of the back of the eye, the retina consists of photoreceptor cells—the rods and cones—which contain the light-sensitive substance known as rhodopsin. When light enters the eye and excites the photoreceptors, a pattern is produced on the retina that is interpreted by the brain as a visual image.

The rods are responsible for nighttime vision, while the cones are responsible for daytime and color vision. The retinal pigmented epithelium (RPE) is a single layer of cells that plays a critical role in vision by processing incoming light rays. This layer of cells absorbs light adjacent to the rods and cones, stores and converts vitamin A, and engulfs discarded pieces of the rods and cones. The RPE rests on a transparent membrane called Bruch's membrane, which separates it from the choroid. The blood supply for the RPE, the choriocapillaris, is just on the other side of Bruch's membrane and is part of the choroid. The choroid supplies oxygen and other nutrients to the RPE photo-receptors.

Optic Nerve

The optic nerve is what lets the brain know just what the eye sees.

Imagine a coaxial cable that carries a TV image from a video camera to a video recorder and manages to make sure that everything that the camera "sees" is faithfully recorded, down to the most minute detail or subtle blend of colors. Now imagine something a whole lot more complicated than that: The optic nerve consists of approximately 1.2 million separate wires or nerve fibers. If any of those nerve fibers are damaged, your vision is also damaged.

Optic neuritis is a condition in which the optic nerves become inflamed and swollen. When this happens, you could wind up with blurry or double vision, headaches, or dim vision—as if someone had turned down the lights or bleached the colors out of what you are seeing. Luckily, optic neuritis usually heals itself.

Extraocular Muscles

The extraocular muscles allow you to move your eyes and gaze in every direction. There are six different muscles attached to the sclera of each eye, and they are all controlled and coordinated by nerves arising from the brain.

Sometimes a faulty nerve connection makes it difficult—or impossible—for the eyes to move together smoothly and properly. The result is a condition known as strabismus, in which one eye appears to "turn" in or out, up or down. It occurs in about 3 percent of all children. But if it is treated early, the deviating eye can retain good vision.

When strabismus is first noticed, the child must have a thorough eye exam to determine the cause of the deviated eye. Quite often, glasses will help solve the problem. Patching the strong eye may build up the strength in the weak or "lazy" eye. Sometimes surgery can be performed on the eye muscles to straighten the eyes and allow them to work together.

Lacrimal Gland

Located just under the bony rim above the eye, this gland produces the tears that wash over the eye's surface. The tears are spread evenly across the eye by the eyelids and are then collected at the inner corners. They drain away through tiny holes in the eyelid margin. From there they travel into the nasolacrimal sac and into the nasolacrimal duct, a long tube connecting the inner corner of the eye socket with the inside of the nose. This connection explains why eyedrops placed in the eye can produce a bitter taste in the throat within a few minutes.

CHAPTER 2

THE EYE EXAM
PUTTING YOUR VISION TO THE TEST

A doctor holds up three fingers during a preinduction physical and asks, "How many fingers do you see?"
"One!" answers the recruit.
"Close enough," replies the doctor. "Welcome to the army."

Thousands of years ago, the "accepted" eye test was to stare up into the night sky at the Big Dipper. You were looking for Alcor, the second star in the handle. Right next to it—in astronomical terms, at least—is its optical double, Mizar. If you could see them as two separate stars, your vision was considered to be adequate.

Today, instead of looking up at a pair of stars 88 light-years away (that's 528,000,000,000,000 miles, give or take a trillion or so), we use an eye chart 20 feet away. Although it lacks the drama of staring up into the night skies, the modern method is more convenient. It doesn't require you to miss any of your late-night TV shows, and you don't have to worry about air pollution reducing your visibility.

It's also at least a smidgen more accurate.

Accuracy is a lot more important today than it was thou-

sands of years ago, because now if the eye doctor finds something wrong with your vision, something can be done to correct it.

But first the doctor has to determine precisely how good
your vision is.

Charting Distance Vision

If you have 20/20 vision, you have average or normal vision—not perfect vision mind you, just average vision. The 20/
20 designation simply means that you can see at 20 feet what the
average person can see at 20 feet. Many people have vision better than 20/20.

To determine what your numbers are, most eye doctors use
the Snellen chart. It has lines of letters on it that start out large at
the top and end up small at the bottom. The 20/20 line is near
the bottom of the chart.

The chart is usually placed 20 feet away from you, and if
you can read the 20/20 line, you are considered to have good
vision.

But let's suppose that you can't read the letters on the 20/20
line, but you can make out the letters on the 20/40 line, which is
three lines above it. That means that you can see at 20 feet what
those with normal vision can see at 40 feet. You have 20/40 vision.

Or let's assume your vision is very sharp and you can make
out the 20/15 line, which is even smaller than the 20/20 line. That
means you can see at 20 feet what someone with normal vision
sees at 15 feet. You have 20/15 vision.

What if all you could see was the large E on top of the Snellen chart? Then your vision would be 20/400. You'd be seeing at
20 feet what a person with normal vision can see at 400.

Thanks to today's corrective lens technology, having less
than 20/20 vision is rarely a major problem. The problems begin
if and when the vision cannot be corrected to 20/20 *with* glasses
or contact lenses. There are people, for example, who can barely
read that 20/400 Snellen E with their naked eyes, but once they
put on their glasses or contact lenses they can pass the eye test

for a driver's license. They may be blind without glasses, but not with them. The legal definition of blindness, by the way, is vision that cannot be corrected to better than 20/200.

Can You Read the Fine Print?

Near vision is tested separately using a printed card, known as a *Jaeger card*, with rows of small type on it. The card is held 14 inches away from the eyes and the patient is asked to read the smallest line possible. Being able to read J2 or J3 means you can read most fine print. A patient who can read the J1 line—which is in smaller type than a telephone book—has great near vision.

While there are people who can read even smaller type, it's not really worth redesigning the Jaeger card just to measure their ability. After all, you are at the eye doctor's to find out if anything is wrong with your eyes, and if so, to get it corrected. The doctor isn't going to do anything for clear vision—whether it be good, great, or fantastic—except congratulate you and give you some hints on keeping it that way.

One further point about near vision. Once you enter your forties, you will probably need reading glasses. Unless, of course, you are nearsighted. Some nearsighted people can still read fine print as they get older, although they sometimes have to take off their regular glasses to do it.

A Study in Contrasts

A growing number of doctors are also testing for visual contrast sensitivity using the *Vision Contrast Test System* (VCTS).

Contrast sensitivity refers to your ability to see the difference between two objects. Let's say, for example, that you can read the 20/20 line—against a white background. But what if the background were gray? What if the letters were gray, too, but a different shade? And while you can see a black-and-white street sign on a bright, sunny day, can you see it on a cloudy day? Can you see it at dusk?

While the Snellen chart is filled with letters or symbols, the VCTS chart is composed of gray circles. Some circles are solid gray. Others have bars inside printed in different shades of gray. It's up to the person being tested to say whether there's a bar in the circle, and, if so, which way it points.

Testing for contrast sensitivity can also help the doctor spot problems such as amblyopia and more dangerous conditions such as glaucoma and cataracts at an early stage.

A Test of a Different Color

While the VCTS chart measures your ability to distinguish among varying shades of gray, color vision–testing cards test your ability to see anything other than gray.

While some people become color-blind as a result of injuries or degenerative diseases that damage the retina or optic nerve, most color-blind people are born that way. And almost all of those people are men. Approximately 8 percent of all men are color-blind to some extent, whereas less than 0.5 percent of women suffer from the condition.

Being color-blind doesn't always mean that you're watching the world on a black-and-white TV. Usually, color-blind people simply cannot always distinguish certain colors, especially red, green, brown, or gray.

Like the VCTS chart, the standard color vision test consists of a series of circles with numbers or objects inside them. The figures are printed in different colors and may or may not be apparent to the person taking the test.

There is no cure for color blindness, and people who are afflicted with it usually adapt to life quite easily. While they might not know if that flashing light on the road ahead is red, blue, or yellow, they do know that a flashing light means that there is some trouble ahead and that they should drive accordingly. And while they might not be able to tell if the signal light shows red, yellow, or green, they know that the top light means stop, the bottom one means go, and the one in the middle means this is their last chance to go before the stoplight comes on.

Eye Exam Guidelines

Most eye tests are conducted in an eye doctor's office by an eye doctor or by an ophthalmic assistant.

A century or so ago, however, they were usually done by a jeweler in his back room. After all, while it took a lens maker to grind corrective lenses, it took a jeweler to put those lenses into a pair of eyeglass frames that actually fit your face.

But because ophthalmologists and optometrists have long since taken over the field from the jewelers, let's look at what one national organization recommends as part of a complete eye exam.

- A review of the patient's and family's general health and eye health history (because some eye conditions are hereditary)
- An examination of the eye's interior and exterior for signs of eye disease or other general health problems that may show up in the eyes
- A test of ability to see sharply and clearly at near and far distances
- Tests for nearsightedness, farsightedness, astigmatism, and presbyopia
- A check of eye coordination and eye muscle function to be certain the eyes are working together as a team
- A test of the ability to change focus quickly, from far to near and back again
- A glaucoma test

Special Tests for Children

Children should have their first eye exam before they are three and should have all of the above tests plus the following ones:

- A check for indications of crossed eyes or indication that the child is not using one eye
- A depth perception test

- A color vision test
- A motor skills test to check eye-hand-foot coordination
- A test to determine the child's dominant eye
- When indicated by the child's development, behavior, or health history, a series of tests should be conducted to determine whether or not the child's vision skills are developing normally. Such tests may include observation of visual abilities while the child is building with blocks, copying forms on paper, or completing incomplete pictures drawn on paper. These tests are selected on the basis of the child's age level.

Help from High-Tech Equipment

Once upon a time, the only way you could find out which lenses were right for you was to put them on and look through them. And if you had to try on 100 or more different lenses or combinations of lenses to find the right ones . . . well, that's life.

Fortunately, the *Phoropter* simplified the process.

Once an eye doctor has determined that you do need glasses—or contact lenses—the next step is this remarkable machine. It contains more than 100 different lenses in a rotary bank, and the doctor can dial different corrective strengths while asking you: "Which lens lets you see better, A or B? Okay. *Now* which lens is better, A or B," and so on. Eventually you get down to two choices that give you vision so good that you yourself can't tell the difference.

This process is referred to as bracketing. Each decision you make gets you closer and closer to the correct lens. Bracketing is merely a trial-and-error process played by the rules of logic, common sense, and good orderly procedure.

Now using the Phoropter to find the right lens is fine if the patient is capable of understanding what it is that's going on and that it requires making a decision. But what do you do with small children?

The simplest method is to use a *retinoscope*. This device shines a light through the pupil of the eye that is reflected back from the retina. The way the light is reflected back tells the eye doctor what sort of lens is needed. This type of objective measuring system can be used on children or anyone else who can't communicate. It even works with dogs or other animals.

Many doctors also use the retinoscope with all their patients before making the initial Phoropter settings, because it gives them a good idea of what range of lenses to start the bracketing procedure with.

When to See an Ophthalmologist

While optometrists provide a good deal of primary eye care, some conditions require the sort of medical examination, evaluation, and treatment that only an ophthalmologist, a medical doctor who specializes in eye care, can offer. These are the signs to look for:

- Blurry vision that can't be corrected by lenses
- Double vision
- Sudden loss of vision
- Dimming of vision that fades in and out
- Red eye
- Eye pain
- Loss of peripheral or side vision
- Halos (colored rays or circles around lights)
- Crossed, turned, or wandering eye
- Twitching of the eyes or eyelids
- Flashes or streaks of light
- New floaters (spots, strings, or shadows in the visual field)
- Discharge, crusting, or excessive tearing
- Swelling of any part of the eye
- Droopy eyelids
- Bulging of one or both eyes
- Difference in the apparent size of the eyes or in pupil size
- Diabetes

More and more eye doctors are investing in an automatic type of retinoscope called an *autorefractor*. By sending out laser beams and measuring how they are reflected back from the retina, the machine automatically finds the right prescription and prints it out. But while it can come close and is especially helpful for dealing with small children, it's not always 100 percent accurate. Most doctors who use an autorefractor put their patients on the Phoropter afterward to fine-tune and double-check the lens selection.

Making the autorefractor part of the normal eye examina-

Iridology:
An Eye Exam for Believers Only

When the noted nineteenth-century British biologist Thomas H. Huxley said that "a little knowledge is dangerous," he might have been talking about Agnus Peczely. It was Peczely, an obscure Hungarian physician, who first enunciated the basic principles of iridology over a century ago.

Peczely said that almost all bodily diseases could be diagnosed by studying the minute details of the iris of the eye. The concept does make more sense than trying to foretell the future by studying the entrails of a sacrificial chicken, but not much.

It is true that some diseases, such as diabetes, high blood pressure, and atherosclerosis, can be detected by examining the eye. But Peczely took this interesting bit of diagnostic trivia and tried to base a new science on it, the pseudoscience of iridology. It made about as much sense as diagnosing character traits through phrenology, the study of the shape of bumps on a person's head, which was also popularized in the nineteenth century.

In spite of the absurdity of these examinations, a cult of ocular diagnosticians began to flourish, particularly in central Europe. Early in this century, iridology was introduced in the United States, and it has been with us ever since. It is now primarily, but not exclusively, within the domain of a small group of chiropractors. Magazine articles, television programs, and newspaper articles have heightened public awareness of this supposed diagnostic method. An attempt to achieve further respectability for iridology was made by wrapping it in the mantle of holistic health.

tion routine can shorten an average eye exam by 5 or 10 minutes. This saves time for everyone and lets the doctor see more patients.

Now let's look at some of the other test equipment an eye doctor might use during an eye test.

A *keratometer* measures the curvature of the cornea. While used primarily for determining what contact lenses a person needs, it is also used after cataract and cornea transplant operations to monitor astigmatism.

A *slit lamp* is a large microscope that lets a doctor examine

Iridologists believe that the iris, the colored part of the eye, serves as a sort of dashboard for the body—complete with warning lights, gauges, and dials. They also believe that they can read these warning lights, gauges, and dials to diagnose problems of the entire body. Aside from the fact that this approach simply doesn't work, many iridologists even disagree with one another as to what part of the iris represents what part of the body. What one iridologist considers to be an indicator of kidney disease may be viewed by another as evidence of a torn kneecap.

For the iridologist, every fleck, spot, color variation, elevation, and depression in the iris is presumed to have diagnostic significance.

Iridologists are fond of diagnosing vague and medieval-sounding diseases such as uterine catarrh, prolapse of the transverse colon, abdominal plethora, lymphatic-rheumatic-tubercular constitution, and all sorts of other mysterious maladies that you will not find listed in any medical dictionary. Most iridologists also just happen to sell the remedies for the diseases they diagnose.

There have been a number of genuine scientific tests of the accuracy of iridology diagnosis. Iridologists were given an opportunity to diagnose people whose medical histories had already been well documented by more boring, but accurate, medical tests. How did the iridologists do? Well, let's just say that no one has yet seen a need to add iridology to the curriculum of Harvard Medical School.

the front of the eye and look for corneal problems, infections, and cataracts.

An *ophthalmoscope* lets the doctor look inside the eye to see if there are any diseases or problems such as vitreous floaters or retinal detachments. It was the development of the ophthalmoscope in Germany in the nineteenth century that marked the beginning of modern ophthalmology.

A *tonometer* tests the intraocular pressure, the pressure produced by fluid inside the eye. High eye pressure is a sign of glaucoma, which can lead to blindness if it isn't detected early and treated. Some tonometers have a small probe that actually touches the surface of the eye, while others shoot a puff of air into the eye to measure the pressure.

More and more eye doctors—both optometrists and ophthalmologists—are investing in *cameras* to photograph the inside and outside of the eye. The pictures give the doctor more time to study the eye and look for abnormalities. By letting the doctor document and compare changes from examination to examination, photographs allow more potentially dangerous conditions to be spotted and dealt with earlier.

A *tangent screen* is used to test peripheral vision—how much you can see happening on your sides while you are looking straight ahead.

With so many ways to precisely measure your vision and screen for possible abnormalities, eye doctors will never have to rely on that old standby—a clear night and a starry sky—again. And there's no reason for you to remain in the dark about your eyesight any longer, either.

CHAPTER 3

GLASSES
BRINGING THE WORLD INTO FOCUS

"Oh, Grandma," gushed Little Red Riding Hood, "what big eyes you have!"
"All the better to see you with, my dear," smirked the wolf.

"Little Red Riding Hood"

Despite the fairy tales, the size of our eyes has very little to do with how well we see. We don't need big eyes. But most of us will—or already do—need big lenses in front of them. In fact, half of all Americans wear glasses, and if you just look at the population aged 45 or older, the number jumps to 95 percent.

While this population includes a lot of different types of people, it's interesting to note that every president of the United States has worn glasses, all the way back to George Washington. Some presidents wore them only in the privacy of their office with the door closed. Others switched to contact lenses.

Even our two youngest presidents wore glasses. John Kennedy, who was elected president at age 43, wore reading glasses, although he rarely let himself be photographed wearing them. Theodore Roosevelt, who was elected vice-president at age 42 and became president shortly before his 43rd birthday (when President William McKinley was assassinated), was usually seen wearing his glasses.

The aging process that makes reading glasses necessary strikes everyone, regardless of race, creed, religion, prestige, or income. And it strikes us all at about the same time, too—in the early forties.

Once you get into your forties, the lenses of your eyes lose their flexibility and need outside help to focus for reading or close work. We'll look at the reasons why in a minute. But first let's take a brief look at the history of eyeglasses, which are also known as glasses, spectacles, specs, magnifiers, and even crutches for your eyes.

Da Vinci Started It All

As with so many other great ideas, Leonardo da Vinci is credited with first coming up with the concept of using magnifying lenses to see better. As technology improved, so did the idea, and the early hand-held magnifying lenses evolved into monocles, which could be held firmly in front of an eye by dint of a dutiful squint.

Since no one can squint all the time without developing a charley horse of the cheek, people kept their monocle on a ribbon pinned to their clothing so that it was always close at hand, even when not close at eye.

Monocles were followed by the lorgnette, two monocle lenses wired together and held to the face with a handle. In the 1600s, craftsmen started joining the two lenses together with a spring-type bridge that held the glasses on the nose.

In 1728 or thereabouts, a London optician named Edward Scarlett invented eyeglasses with temple pieces. But they weren't designed to hang on the ears. Instead they stayed in place by gripping the head in a migrainelike embrace.

It's worth remembering that patent laws weren't very rigid 250 years ago, and it's hard to prove that any one person was the first to do anything. The odds are that reading glasses—like the wheel, shoes, and rock and roll—were an idea whose time had come. They were probably developed by a number of different clever people working independently.

Take, for example, the case of bifocals. Tradition states that Benjamin Franklin should get the credit for that one, because he crafted glasses that combined an upper lens for distance vision and a lower one for near vision. Franklin first wrote of his invention in 1784. But London opticians had been experimenting with the idea for more than 20 years by that time, and other people had been writing about the concept since at least 1716.

But regardless of who first actually made that optical breakthrough or any of the others, those early glasses were designed to do the same thing Leonardo da Vinci's magnifying lenses were designed to do centuries earlier—correct a few of nature's mistakes.

The Most Common Vision Problems

Still thinking about the human eye as a camera, picture a series of lenses at the front of the eyeball that bend light and focus it into an image recorded on the retina in the back of the eye.

If the eye is perfectly shaped, and the distance between the cornea (lens) and the retina (film) is exactly right, the image projected on the retina is in perfect focus—crisp, clear, and sharp. That's exactly the sort of image that about half the population below the age of 40 sees naturally. But the other half of the population doesn't see it correctly, and here's where glasses come in.

Glasses—and contact lenses, which we will deal with in the next chapter—are primarily used to correct four different but depressingly common vision problems: nearsightedness, farsightedness, astigmatism, and presbyopia. To complicate matters, some people suffer from two or more of the four. In each of the four, however, the lenses in the glasses have to compensate for the eyes' natural limitations.

Nearsightedness

For nearsighted, or myopic, people, the world is a blurry place for one of two reasons. Either their eyes are too long or the focusing power of their eyes is too strong.

Light first carries an image through the cornea and then through the flexible crystalline lens behind it. Eye muscles bend and stretch the crystalline lens to bring objects into focus. (As you get older, you naturally lose lens flexibility and develop presbyopia, which will be covered later in this chapter.) The lens also acts as a projector. It projects the image on the retina in much the same way a movie projector puts an image on a screen. With nearsighted people, however, the lens is too powerful, and the image comes into sharp focus before it can reach the retina.

With a slide projector and a portable screen, you can demonstrate the process. Set up the screen and project a slide on it. Make sure you have the image in pinpoint focus. Now move the screen back a few feet.

The image that reaches the screen now is blurry because the screen—just like the retina—is behind the point of perfect focus. To get the image back into focus, you have three choices:

1. Move the screen, which would be the same as moving the retina of the eye.
2. Refocus the projector's lens. Some people manage to refocus by squinting, which puts a little more concentrated focusing power into their eye, but squinting becomes rather tiresome after a while.
3. Add an additional lens in the form of glasses. Properly prescribed and made, lenses will change the distance the image travels to make sure it ends up on the retina in perfect focus.

A myopic person doesn't always need glasses to see everything, just things that are far away. Near objects can often be focused on quite easily.

Myopia, or nearsightedness, is the single most common focusing or refractive problem. Most of the people you see wearing glasses are myopic. While about half of all the people with myopia have focusing systems that are just too powerful, the other half have eyeballs that are just a tad too long. The cornea, which is the most powerful lens of the eye, works just fine, but the retina isn't where it's supposed to be.

Let's assume that the lens on our slide projector was built to focus on a screen exactly 20 feet away. But when the projector is set up and locked into place in the projection booth, the screen is 22 feet away—and cannot be moved. The lens is doing its job, but the screen is in the wrong place. So whether you were born with a focusing system just a tad too strong or an eyeball just a smidgen too long, the effect is the same. You need glasses.

Farsightedness

Now let's look at the world through the eye of a farsighted person, a person with hyperopia. Instead of focusing the image right on the retina, the farsighted person's lens system focuses the image behind the retina.

The image reaches the retina before it comes into focus. Take the projector and screen and set it up again so that the image is in perfect, pinpoint focus. Now instead of moving the screen backward, move it forward 2 feet.

The picture is out of focus.

While a nearsighted person needs glasses that will move the focal point back, a farsighted person needs glasses to move the focal point forward. If you have farsightedness, or hyperopia, you can see distant things reasonably well. Your problems begin when you have to look at something close up.

Only about 10 percent of the people who wear glasses have to do so because they are farsighted. Like their nearsighted cousins, hyperopic people can be farsighted for two different reasons. Either the focusing power of the eyes is too weak or their eyeballs are a bit too short.

Again, glasses can correct either problem.

Astigmatism

While people with myopia and hyperopia have problems with the focal length of their lenses, people with astigmatism have problems with the shape of their cornea and lens. There are three things to remember about this.

1. A "perfect" eye is perfectly round.
2. An astigmatic eye isn't perfectly round.
3. No one has a perfectly round eye.

(continued on page 28)

Refractive Errors of the Eye

NORMAL VISION

In an emmetropic eye, one that is properly rounded, the image is focused directly onto the surface of the retina and can be seen normally, in perfect focus.

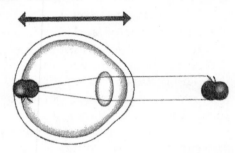

MYOPIA

In a myopic, or nearsighted, eye, the image comes into perfect focus before it reaches the retina. By the time it gets to the retina it is slightly out of focus, producing a blurry image. The situation can be "corrected" with a minus, or concave, lens that compensates for the fact that the eye is slightly elongated. The corrective lens, coupled with the eye's own lens system, focuses the image directly on the retina.

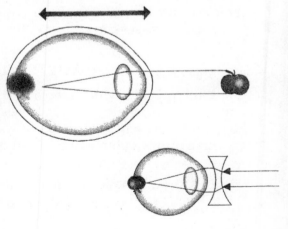

HYPEROPIA

In a hyperopic, or far-sighted, eye, the image reaches the retina before it comes into perfect focus, producing a blurry image. This condition can be "corrected" by using a plus, or convex, lens that compensates for the fact that the eye is not long enough. The corrective lens, coupled with the eye's own lens system, focuses the image directly on the retina.

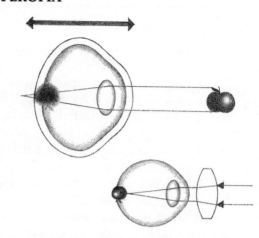

ASTIGMATISM

An astigmatic eye is not properly rounded. As a result, different parts of an image may come into focus before or after it reaches the retina. An astigmatic lens is used to "correct" this situation. This type of lens is made to compensate for the irregular shape of the eye.

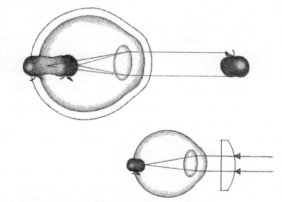

PRESBYOPIA

Once people pass the age of 40, they start to develop presbyopia. The lens loses its youthful elasticity and its ability to focus on close objects. People with this condition become slightly hyperopic, or farsighted. Presbyopia can be "corrected" with a plus, or convex, lens that would only be required for reading or other close work.

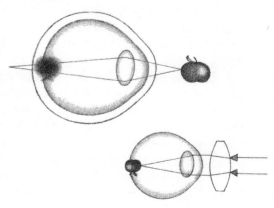

Everyone has a bit of astigmatism in either the lens or the cornea—or both. It's a matter of degree.

The astigmatic eye has at least two different curves, and instead of looking like a baseball, it can—in some cases—be shaped more like a football, or a basketball with a beer belly.

In most people the degree of astigmatism is usually so slight that there is no problem. But if the astigmatism is bad enough to cause blurry vision, glasses are needed.

Why does an astigmatism cause blurry vision?

A slide projector's lens is rounded so that the different light images that hit it anywhere on its surface will all travel the same distance to reach the focal point—the screen. What's more, the images will all make the trip in the same time.

Now imagine focusing through a glass football. Because it's not perfectly round, the images hitting it at different spots on the surface will have different distances to travel to reach the focal point. As a result, some of what you see will appear to be in perfect focus, and some of it will appear distorted.

For a more extreme example, let's look at a mirror in a carnival funhouse. Since the surface is distorted—bent out of shape—light hitting it will reflect back distorted images. Depending on the curves in the mirror, your "mirror image" could show you with short stubby legs, a belly the size of a truck, and a neck like a giraffe's.

Of course, if you actually do look like that, your image in a distorted—astigmatic—mirror could make you look sexier than your favorite TV star. As proved by countless movies and magic acts, you can do amazing things with mirrors.

Luckily, most corneal astigmatism is not as exaggerated as that found in a funhouse mirror, but even a slight degree of astigmatism is enough to cause problems—a wide variety of problems.

Depending on the shape your eyes are in, part of what you see could be perfectly focused while other parts could be perfectly fuzzy. That's because part of the image could come through the cornea and crystalline lens and wind up in focus right on your retina, and another part could wind up just in front of the retina or just behind it.

Astigmatic eyes could also focus both images in front of or behind the retina, or partially in front of and partially behind, or . . .

You get the idea. The possibilities are enough to make your eyes ache just thinking about them. The important thing to remember is that there is a solution. The distorted astigmatic image that hits your retina can be corrected with glasses ground in curves to compensate for the curves nature threw your eyes.

What does an astigmatic person see? Go back to your slide projector, turn it on and focus it, and then place a clear drinking glass just in front of the lens. Now move it around and see what the images on the screen look like. You can also go to a carnival funhouse and look at yourself in the mirrors.

Or go to the library, check out an art book, and study some of the paintings of El Greco. Many people believe that Spain's most famous Greek painter—*El Greco* means "the Greek"—had an uncorrected astigmatism, which got worse as he got older. If so, this would explain why the figures in his paintings are so long and thin.

Presbyopia

While myopia, hyperopia, and astigmatism happen to only some of the people, presbyopia happens to all of the people—if they live long enough. It's a natural part of growing older.

The eye has a remarkable mechanism for changing its power—or focal length—to look at something close, such as the page of this book. The eye can do this because the crystalline lens behind the cornea stretches.

When you are reading or looking at your watch, a reflex contracts one of the eye muscles, causing the crystalline lens to automatically fatten a bit. This brings a close object into sharp focus. This is called the accommodation reflex.

As you get older, though, the crystalline lens loses its flexibility. It's a gradual process. While you once might have been able to read a phone number out of a phone book as soon as you opened it, you may notice that you have to squint a bit to bring the fine print into focus.

At a certain point—usually in your early forties—you'll have to trade in your squint for a pair of reading glasses, or give up on phone books completely.

Presbyopia has struck again.

It will continue to strike, reducing your eye's elasticity year after year so that you will need even stronger reading glasses until, at about age 65, the process stops. Your eyes won't change much after that.

While presbyopia does strike everyone, it doesn't leave everyone needing reading glasses. If you have just the right amount of nearsightedness, you may be able to simply take off your regular glasses to read. It's like having built-in reading glasses. Of course, distance vision will still be blurry for near-sighted folks, but you could be the envy of all your friends when you take *off* your glasses to read the restaurant menu or the fine print in the phone book.

Special Glasses for Special Needs

Conventional eyeglasses are made to correct one vision problem and as a result have only one power. No matter which part of the lens you look through, the power, or magnification, is pretty much the same. But presbyopic people need a different power for near vision than they need for distance vision.

Bifocals solve this problem by providing two separate lenses for each eye. The upper one is for distance vision and the lower one is for near vision.

Trifocal glasses incorporate three lenses: an upper lens for distance, a lower lens for reading or close work, and an intermediate lens for the middle distances. Trifocals are especially useful for typists and piano players. While bifocals and trifocals are convenient, they can take a little getting used to, since your vision "jumps" as your eyes cross the line between the lenses.

That line can also be a major ego problem. Many people look at bifocals and trifocals as something that only old people wear, and are willing to put up with all sorts of inconvenience, annoyance, embarrassment, and outright danger rather than have people think they are getting old.

One way around the line problem is with "seamless" bifocals. They blend the distance and close-up portions of the lens without the telltale bifocal line. These can work very well and should be considered by those who are annoyed—or embarrassed—by ordinary bifocals.

Because they are more difficult to grind accurately, they do cost more than conventional bifocals, but many people consider them worth the extra expense. Of course, if you've already gotten used to regular bifocals or trifocals, it may be difficult to adjust to the different focusing system of the seamless bifocal.

Another way to solve this problem is with two different pairs of glasses. Not only is it inconvenient, it is also more expensive, because you need to have two complete pairs of glasses.

Safety Glasses

All prescription glasses are required by law to be impact resistant and meet specific safety requirements. Under the regulations, if a ⅝-inch-diameter steel ball bearing were to be dropped on one of the lenses from a height of 50 inches, no fragments should fly into the eye.

The standards for industrial safety glasses are even tougher. Such lenses must be at least 3 millimeters thick and capable of withstanding the impact of a 1-inch ball bearing dropped from 50 inches. In addition, the frames must be both sturdy and flame resistant.

Either glass or plastic lenses may be used for either regular or safety glasses. Plastic lenses do scratch more easily than glass lenses, but because they weigh only half as much as glass, many people find them more comfortable.

Today, however, the development of lighter-weight glass lenses and more scratch-resistant plastic ones is minimizing the differences between the two types of lens.

Sunglasses

Sunglasses are a lot older than reading glasses. They may even be older than glass.

Unknown centuries ago, Eskimos started making an early form of sunshade to prevent snow blindness. They would carve an eye "mask" out of wood and put in narrow slits to look through. The slits gave them enough of a view to work with, and because they were so narrow, they blocked out the glare that could have caused snow blindness.

Five Myths about Glasses

There are myths about four-leaf clovers, dogs named Rover, golden jars, and shooting stars, so, of course, there are myths about glasses, too. And many of them make as much sense as the one about four-leaf clovers bringing luck. Here are five of them:

1. Wearing glasses will strengthen your eyes. Glasses don't change your eyes at all. What they do affect is your vision, by giving your brain a clearer image of what your eyes see.

2. Wearing glasses will weaken your eyes. See myth number 1.

3. Wearing glasses will make you "addicted" to wearing glasses. The only habit that wearing glasses develops is the habit of actually seeing what's going on around you—and seeing it clearly and distinctly.

4. If you have a lot of headaches, you need glasses. If you have a lot of headaches, it means that you have a lot of headaches. Because the vast majority of headaches are tension- or stress-related, the odds are you are under a lot of stress. A small number of headaches can be classified as migraine headaches. High blood pressure, sinus infections, allergies, and tumors can also cause headaches. Rarely will people develop headaches because they need glasses. Those who do are usually farsighted and develop headaches when they read for a long time without wearing glasses. When they stop reading or start using glasses, the headaches will usually disappear.

5. Glasses make you smarter. Obviously a conspiracy started by the people who manufacture glasses, this one is based on appearances. For reasons better dealt with by practitioners of cultural anthropology than of ophthalmology, we tend to think that people who wear glasses look smarter than people who don't. One possible reason is that we associate glasses with people who have weak eyes because they read so much (see myth number 2). But wearing glasses can also make you appear smarter by giving you more time to think. Ask people who wear glasses a hard question and they will very likely take the glasses off and clean them before answering you. They aren't cleaning their glasses because the glasses need cleaning, or to see the problem—or you—more clearly. They're doing it to give themselves a few extra seconds to think of an answer, time they wouldn't have if they didn't find something to do with their hands while they were thinking.

Ancient Tibetans wove fine horsehair into a kind of sun visor. And more than 2,000 years ago, the Chinese wore tinted lenses because of the good luck they supposedly brought—and the bad luck they supposedly prevented. Chinese judges, for example, wore smoked-glass lenses to conceal their thoughts from defendants.

Tinted lenses were worn in the United States in the early 1800s, but they didn't really take off until the first planes did. It was in the 1920s that the U.S. Army Air Corps started looking seriously at sunglasses as a way to help fliers cope with high-altitude glare. The sunglasses market has been flying high ever since.

While many people look at sunglasses as a fashion accessory, they do also provide important visual comfort and protection by cutting down on the amount of visible light, glare, and ultraviolet (UV) radiation that reaches the eyes. The amount of light that does get through is determined by the "transmission factor" of the sunglasses.

Generally speaking, no more than 30 percent of outdoor bright sunlight should be transmitted to the eyes. But if you are at the beach or on the ski slopes, where the sunlight is brighter and there is a high glare factor, a transmission factor of just 10 to 15 percent may be preferable. Manufacturers often attach a tag to their sunglasses listing the transmission factor.

Depending on what you are going to be doing, you might prefer one of the following types of sunglasses:

● Gradient density sunglasses are dark at the top, tapering to clear at the bottom.

● Double-gradient density sunglasses are dark at the top and at the bottom and lighter in the center. They are especially useful for driving, boating, or any other situation where there is a great deal of overhead light and low-level glare.

● Reflective sunglasses have a thin metallic coating that reduces the amount of light that reaches the eyes by reflecting it away.

- Polarizing lenses eliminate vertical glare. They are very effective and often very comfortable.
- UV lenses filter out ultraviolet rays.
- Photochromic lenses adjust to the amount of light hitting them by automatically becoming darker in bright sunlight and turning clear again when the light dims. While many people are happy with automatic sunglasses, others find the process bothersome and too slow.

More and more researchers are tying excessive UV exposure to a number of serious eye problems such as cataracts and macular degeneration (see chapters 8 and 12). While more work needs to be done to prove this connection, if it is true, glasses that screen out UV light may help slow down these sight-threatening conditions.

In the meantime, what should you do about UV light?

- Be aware that a connection may very well exist. It hasn't been proved yet, but it hasn't been disproved, either. Play it safe, but don't let it drive you crazy with worry.
- Be aware that there are a lot of promoters out there trying to put the fear of God into all of us about the disastrous effects of UV light. And once they have us thoroughly cowed, they pull out their complete line of UV glasses.
- Take some reasonable precautions. Try not to face directly into the sun; wear sunglasses if you spend a lot of time in bright sunlight.

Some research is being done now with sun-screening eye-drops, which would block out potentially harmful UV rays. The drops would last for several hours and would be reapplied as needed. But even if they do work, they won't reduce glare or brightness. Sunglasses will still be around.

Just as sunglasses come in different styles, they also come in different colors. But no matter what the current fashion gurus might dictate, you don't want to look out at the world through rose-colored glasses—or pink, blue, or purple ones.

Neutral gray or "smoke" is the best color. It gives the best color perception and the least distortion. It is also the most difficult tint to produce, and as a result, it is only available in better-quality, more expensive sunglasses.

Green- and brown-tinted lenses are also good choices, but forget the silly ones designed by people who think color-coordinating your sunglasses and your shoelaces makes an important fashion statement. Pink, blue, purple, orange, rose, yellow, striped, and polka-dot sunglass lenses look better on a store dummy than they do on you—and are about as useful.

Sunglasses: How to Check for Quality

While sunglass style is important to your ego, quality is important to your vision. But in today's marketplace, where a designer label can often double, triple, or even quadruple the profit margin on an item, a high-class label is no guarantee of high-class quality, or for that matter, of any quality whatsoever. So here is a simple way to judge the quality of a pair of sunglasses:

- Examine them against the light for scratches, streaks, bubbles, blurs, or other flaws.

- Hold them at arm's length and focus on an object with strong vertical and horizontal lines, such as a door or window frame. Move the glasses up, down, and sideways. If the lines waver, then there's a distortion in the lens. (This test works only on nonprescription lenses. With prescription lenses, some distortion may be built into the lens for corrective purposes.)

- Put the glasses down on a white surface to check that the lenses are of equal color and density. Badly matched lenses can affect depth perception and cause eye fatigue.

CHAPTER 4

CONTACT LENSES
FINDING WHAT'S RIGHT FOR YOU

Men seldom make passes
At girls who wear glasses.

Dorothy Parker

The invention of eyeglasses made it possible for millions of people to see the world clearly. The invention of contact lenses—corrective lenses placed directly on the eyes—made it possible for them to do so without anyone knowing that they need any help in seeing clearly.

Opinions about contact lenses vary widely. They've been hailed as a major improvement over glasses; they've also been derided as merely an ego-gratifying cosmetic device. Actually, the truth is somewhere in the middle, although its position shifts slightly with each person who wears contact lenses because each person's needs are different.

As he did with glasses, Leonardo da Vinci also gets credit for creating the contact lenses concept. It developed out of his discovery, in 1508, that when he stuck his head in a large bowl of water, the pressure of the liquid pressing against his eyes cleared his distorted vision. While it was not one of his more practical discoveries (at least not at the time), he recorded his observations in one of his notebooks.

Some 300 years later, English physicist Thomas Young replaced the bowl of water with a water-filled tube and placed a lens at one end of it. He got a sharp image, and it was a more practical discovery than Leonardo's—but not by much. It wasn't until the 1940s that someone came up with a true contact lens that really worked.

Those early lenses were made of glass and covered the entire front surface of the eye. Although they did sharpen vision, they were so uncomfortable that people couldn't stand wearing them for more than a few hours.

The second generation of contact lenses arrived in the late 1940s and early 1950s. Designed to fit on top of the cornea, they were smaller, rounder, and made out of plastic. While they did produce reasonably good vision for many people, they moved up and down with each blink, were uncomfortable, and could be worn only a limited number of hours a day. If the irritation or pain didn't tell the wearer when it was time to remove them, blurry vision did.

Perfecting the Modern Lens

During the 1950s and 1960s, researchers tried different materials to make contact lenses more comfortable and also redesigned the lenses by tapering and smoothing the edges.

Doctors and contact lens makers finally figured out that while large and heavy lenses caused eye and eyelid irritation, the major source of eye pain from wearing contact lenses was oxygen starvation. The lenses were blocking the normal supply of air to the cornea. And the less air the cornea received, the more pain it generated.

As they continued their investigations, researchers also learned that small amounts of oxygen are normally dissolved in tears. Because the cornea is constantly lubricated by tears, and

Who Wears Contacts?

More than 20 million Americans wear contact lenses, according to eye care industry statistics. Nearly 70 percent of them are women. By comparison, more than 114 million Americans wear glasses.

Due to increased problems with infections and the resulting bad publicity, the number of contact lens wearers has actually declined since 1984, when nearly 25 million Americans wore lenses.

Of those wearing contact lenses today, nearly 12 million wear soft daily-wear lenses; 4 million wear rigid gas-permeable lenses; 3.5 million wear soft extended-wear lenses; and 1.5 million wear hard lenses.

The cosmetic benefit of not having to wear glasses as well as improved self-image and self-confidence are the most common reasons people give for switching to contact lenses, according to Bausch & Lomb, a leading eye care products manufacturer.

The company says there are also ten other frequently mentioned benefits.

- Improved peripheral vision
- No eyeglass barrier to interfere with the line of sight
- Lenses move with the eyes, providing more natural vision with less distortion.
- Better depth perception
- Lenses are invisible on the eye, so they can never go out of style.
- Convenient for an active lifestyle
- Ease participation in sports and other physical activities
- Lenses don't fog up or get wet in the rain.
- No eyeglass frames to slide off the nose, hurt the ears, or get hot in the summer
- No red marks caused by eyeglass frames

since contact lenses actually float on a thin layer of tears, they reasoned that the best way to ease the discomfort would be to find a way to let more tears come into contact with the cornea.

What they had to come up with was a small, smooth, lightweight lens that would not block off the cornea's oxygen supply.

And they succeeded. But just as there is no one pair of eyeglasses that will serve everyone's needs, there is no one perfect
contact lens. Instead, we now have a wide selection to choose
from, all designed for different needs.

Hard Lenses

Hard contact lenses correct vision in two ways.

1. They smooth out any irregular curves on the front part
    of the cornea, providing a new spherical front surface
    for the eye.
2. Like eyeglass lenses, they can also have a prescription
    built into them.

Hard contact lenses can correct nearsightedness, farsightedness, and astigmatism. They can also correct vision in an eye
that has had a cataract operation.

They may also take months of getting used to. At first,
wearers feel as if they have small pebbles in their eyes. After
several weeks or months, they may begin to adapt to the discomfort. But not all do.

Try This Wake-Up Warm-Up for Your Eyes

Don't put your contact lenses in as soon as you wake up. Let
your eyes "breathe" for an hour first.

Consider this a form of warm-up exercise.

In the same way that doing a series of stretches and warm-
ups before a workout loosens up your body and reduces the
chance of muscle aches, giving your eyes an hour to adjust to
being up, open, and focused will reduce the chance of discomfort.

Whether or not you wear your glasses during that hour is up
to you. The important thing is to give your eyes a chance to wake
up. Besides, for most of us, having the world slightly out of focus
from time to time helps us keep it and our place in it in proper
perspective.

Soft Lenses

In the late 1950s, Otto Wichterle, a Czech doctor, introduced a new soft, flexible, and water-absorbing plastic material for making contact lenses—2-hydroxyethyl methacrylate. Lenses made from the new material and its derivatives contain between 25 and 75 percent water. The water can come either from the wearer's normal tears or from the solution the lenses are stored in.

Like hard contact lenses, the soft lenses also float on a layer of tears. But they are flexible and larger, and they let the cornea breathe more normally.

The larger diameter means that the top and bottom edges remain underneath the eyelids as long as the lenses are in the eyes. Thus there is less edge for the eyelid to rub against every time the wearer blinks.

All of these qualities add up to more comfort.

Unlike hard lenses, which require weeks or even months of limited daily use to build up "wearing time," soft lenses are often comfortable the first time they are put in. People typically say that they can feel their soft lenses at the start, but add that the sensation is not an uncomfortable one. After a few weeks of wearing soft lenses all day every day, most wearers barely notice them at all. No wonder millions of people have traded in their glasses for two tiny, flexible disks.

Extended-Wear Lenses

The next logical development after a soft contact lens that could be worn comfortably all day was a soft contact lens that could be worn comfortably all day and all night, and all day and all night, and so on.

Researchers knew that such a lens would have to be thinner than a regular soft contact lens, have a higher water content, and allow even more oxygen to pass through its surface.

When extended-wear lenses were first introduced in the mid–1970s amid suitable hope, hype, and fanfare, millions of contact lens wearers wanted to try them. The promise of being able to trade those old put-in-take-out-and-clean-every-day contacts for new lenses that could be worn for weeks at a time was hailed as the next best thing to being able to trade old eyes for new.

The celebrating was both enthusiastic and premature. Yes, the new lenses were comfortable, extremely comfortable. They could be left in the eyes for long periods of time without causing any discomfort. And that led to new problems.

Because they were in the eyes for such long periods, any debris that found its way into the tears—such as dirt and natural mineral deposits—wound up on the lens. While some of these deposits could be cleaned off, there was usually some residue left. But even if it could all be removed, that still required taking the lens out more often than many people wanted to.

If they had to take them out all the time, they asked, what was the point of having them?

That was only one problem. The next one was more serious—infections. More and more people got them.

Why?

Like the rest of our body, the human eye is a complex combination of parts, pieces, chemicals, and compounds operating in perfect balance. Change the balance, and . . . well, it's like those old jokes that all end with the punch line: "It's not nice to try to fool Mother Nature."

The eye "knows" when something isn't in perfect balance. It knows when there is a foreign object there. No matter how good a contact lens is for vision, it is not a natural part of the eye. Its very presence can disturb the delicate balance of microbes in and around the eye. And the constant rubbing of the lens can make the cornea susceptible to bacteria.

Not everyone who wears extended-wear contact lenses is destined to develop a corneal infection. But those who do may be left with scarred corneas and decreased vision. Such episodes can, on occasion, even lead to blindness. That's why learning how to wear contact lenses is only part of the process. Learning when *not* to wear them, and when to call your doctor about signs and symptoms, is equally important.

If there is *any* pain, redness, or decreased vision, check with your eye doctor.

No matter what you may have heard, a month of continuous wear without cleaning the lenses is too much. Remove the lenses at least one night a week and give them a good cleaning and disinfecting. Then leave them out overnight. A good cleaning will be almost as beneficial for your lenses as not wearing them for one night will be for your corneas.

If you can wear daily lenses, they may be better for your eyes in the long run than extended-wear lenses. But if extended-wear lenses are the only ones you can comfortably wear, you might consider taking them out each night anyway and treating them like daily-wear lenses.

A Nasty Reaction to Dirty Lenses

Giant papillary conjunctivitis (GPC) is an irritative and possibly allergic reaction to the gunk your contact lenses collect.

Most commonly found in people wearing soft or extended-wear lenses, GPC develops because the material used in those types of lenses tends to attract protein and other foreign material more easily than hard or gas-permeable lenses do. While people wearing the latter types of lenses can also get GPC, their odds of avoiding it are better.

GPC's symptoms are blurred vision, mucus discharge, redness, excessive lens movement, and little bumps (papillae) on the inside of the upper eyelids.

Interestingly, an antiallergy eyedrop, Opticrom, helps relieve symptoms in many patients with GPC. This might suggest that GPC is an allergic reaction. But more likely, mast cells—the cells that contain histamine and other allergic mediators—are stimulated or irritated by the constant rubbing of the contact lens on the inner lining of the upper lids.

Gas-Permeable Lenses

Gas-permeable lenses combine some of the benefits of both hard and soft lenses.

Like hard lenses, they are rigid and durable, and they do not collect a lot of deposits. But like soft lenses, they are made of material that lets more oxygen pass through to the cornea.

While usually not as comfortable as soft lenses, gas-permeable lenses are still much more comfortable than hard lenses, and much, much more easy to get used to.

As technology improves, these lenses are becoming even more comfortable and may be worn for longer and longer stretches. They are already being tested by some doctors as extended-wear lenses.

Disposable Lenses

While disposable contact lenses offer comfort and convenience, there are some drawbacks.

They are extended-wear lenses, made to be thrown away after one or two weeks of wearing. They are not meant to be taken out and cleaned like regular extended-wear lenses, but they do get dirty and can cause infections.

Some people try to save money by cleaning and reusing them. This is not a good idea. Disposable lenses aren't made to be cleaned and disinfected, and you could wind up doing more harm than good.

You might think that disposable contact lenses are much more expensive than nondisposable lenses. But if you have to change lenses every year or so anyway, as do most extended-wear lens wearers, and if you add in the price of cleaning solutions and equipment, the price difference isn't really that great.

Extended Wear—Extended Danger

No matter what the advertisements for extended-wear lenses might say, wearing any contact lenses continuously for more than one week could lead to serious eye problems—including blindness.

After extensive testing, the Food and Drug Administration has determined that people who wear extended-wear contact lenses are five times more likely to develop eye infections than those wearing ordinary lenses that are removed at night. The specific infection looked for in the study is ulcerative keratitis. It can lead to permanent eye damage, even blindness. The condition develops when bacteria grow in the oxygen-starved space between the contact lens and the surface of the eye.

Researchers have found that extended-wear lens wearers are also prone to other eye infections and irritations. So for best results, remove your contact lenses every night and let your eyes sleep in the nude.

Soft Astigmatic Lenses

While most people with astigmatism wear hard or gas-permeable lenses, there are soft lenses available, too. But they don't work for everyone.

Standard contact lenses have the same degree of correction throughout. This means they can rotate on the eye without there being any concern about which edge is "up." Astigmatic lenses, on the other hand, have varying degrees of correction on various parts of the lens surface to compensate for the shape of the section of the eye directly underneath. If these lenses rotated while on the eye, it would be like looking through a different pair of glasses every time you blinked. To prevent this, the bottom edge of each lens is weighted to hold it in place.

Astigmatic soft lenses are costly and hard to fit properly, and they don't always work. But while hard and gas-permeable astigmatic lenses are less expensive and more dependable, not everyone with astigmatism can—or is willing to—adjust to them.

Caring for Your Eyes and Your Contact Lenses

It is important to remember that if contact lenses are not treated properly, they can do more damage than good. Treating them properly includes keeping them clean.

The biggest single reason your lenses get dirty isn't dirt, smog, or even dust in the wind. It's your tears. Like the ocean, tears contain a lot more than just water. They contain mucus, which helps coat the cornea and spread the tears out evenly over the entire surface of the eye. Old, worn-out cells from the surface of the eye also get mixed with the tears, along with dust, dirt, general air pollution, sweat, and—if you wear it—eye makeup.

All of this debris tends to gather at the corner of the eye, where it can harden and turn into what some people call "sand" or grit. If you're wearing contact lenses, some of it sticks to the lens. Failure to clean it off can lead to infections as well as dirty lenses.

Lenses, by the way, are a lot like dishes. The sooner you clean them, the easier they are to clean. Anyone who has ever waited a day or two to scrape dried egg yolk off a plate knows what we mean.

So clean your lenses as soon as you take them out. Just make sure your hands are clean before you go to work on your lenses. Also make sure that the cleaning solutions you use are fresh. Most labels tell you how long a solution is good for after it's been opened. Mark the date on the bottle, and if you haven't finished the bottle by the expiration date, throw it out anyhow.

Once the lenses are clean—be sure to follow the manufacturer's suggestion for the specific lenses you have—the cleaning solution should be thoroughly rinsed off. Soft lenses need to be disinfected with either heat or chemicals. Again, follow the manufacturer's instructions. Hard lenses do not require disinfection, and may be stored either in saline or special soaking solution or kept dry.

Selecting a Lens Cleaner

There are numerous brands of contact lens cleaning solutions. Shop around until you find the one that you like best, then use it every time you take your lenses out.

But please keep this in mind while you are doing your shopping. Regardless of the advertising claims, there are some things that just don't seem to make much sense. One of them is the notion that a single all-purpose contact lens fluid can be equally effective as a cleaning, wetting, and soaking solution.

First, let's consider the nature of soap and other cleaning agents. Such products are designed to dissolve and break up particles of dirt and other foreign matter so they can be rinsed away. But will soap irritate your eyes? We all know the answer to that one, especially if you're going to leave a soap-cleaned lens in your eyes for 8, 10, or 12 hours.

On the other hand, if a soaking solution is gentle enough to go into your eyes without irritating them, how good a job can it be doing at dissolving and breaking up the gunk that collects on your lenses?

There are cleaning solutions and there are soaking solutions. Rinse one off before you use the other.

And no matter what brands you use, follow the directions.

If you ever drop a lens on the floor, into grass, or into the soup, clean it thoroughly before sticking it back on your eye. Remember, though, that putting a lens in your mouth is a great way to get it dirty—not clean. There are bacteria in your mouth that your eyes just can't handle.

Never forget that contact lenses are not natural. Even when they are well cared for, they can still cause or aggravate some eye problems. If your eyes hurt, or if they are red, watering more than usual, or unusually sensitive to light, take the lenses out and see your doctor immediately. Any blurring of vision is another warning signal.

Like glasses, contact lenses do not change your natural vision. They just give your brain a clearer image of what your eyes see. Wearing them will not stop, prevent, or even slow down the natural changes your eyes will go through. Nor will it speed them up. At a certain age you will need reading glasses, whether or not you wore glasses or contact lenses in the past.

The Case for the Case

Of course you have to keep your contact lenses clean. That goes without saying.

What still needs to be said, however, is that you have to keep your contact lens case antiseptically clean, too. In fact, doctors are finding that more and more instances of corneal infection among contact lens wearers can be traced to their contact lens cases and the soaking solutions their lenses are stored in.

Contamination is most likely to occur if the soaking solution is not changed daily, or at least every other day. If your lenses are stored continuously for several days or weeks, they should be cleaned and disinfected before you put them back in your eyes. The bacteria that cause many corneal infections grow best in cases that are left closed with soaking solution in them.

The solution in your case should always be dumped out when you put your lenses in your eyes. While you are wearing your lenses, wash out the case thoroughly in hot water and let it air dry, upside down, on a paper towel. Refill with new solution when you put your lenses back in the case.

Choosing the Right Lens

Choosing the right type of contact lens isn't nearly as complicated as choosing a new car, a home, or even what color sweatband to wear with your new passion-pink-and-purple polka-dot sweatpants.

The choice of lenses will be heavily influenced by the type of eye problem you have, your budget, your habits, and your doctor.

Make sure you have a doctor or eye-care professional you are comfortable with, one who has a lot of experience fitting all of the different types of contact lenses.

The fitting process can be long and difficult. Make sure you know what the lenses will cost and how much help the doctor or the doctor's assistant will be in teaching you to put them in and take them out. Many doctors offer an all-inclusive fee covering eye tests, lenses, and "lessons."

In some ways, learning how to use your contact lenses is like learning how to ride a bike. But instead of falling and scraping your knees, you will poke yourself in the eye with your finger a few times. You will also "lose" the lens underneath the eyelid. But don't panic. The lens cannot get back behind the eye. If it's in there, it can be removed.

There are numerous techniques to use with your contacts, and you will have to keep fiddling with a number of them until you find what works best for you. If you keep at it, you will find that putting your lenses in and taking them out takes nearly as little time as putting your glasses on or taking them off.

Many people have more problems getting their lenses out than they do putting them in, especially when there is dust or dirt causing discomfort in the eye. When all else fails, stick your face in a sink full of water, open your eyes and let the lenses float off. Just make sure you have the sink stopper in.

Some Pros and Cons

Hard lenses are the easiest to put in and take out. But they are also more likely to come off at the wrong time—during a sneeze or a cough, for instance. Losing one at a critical moment and having to crawl around on the floor looking for it can be very embarrassing. It is also easier for dirt or dust to get underneath a hard contact lens.

Hard lenses and gas-permeable lenses are the most economical and most durable. Not only are they cheaper than soft lenses, they can last up to ten years. Soft lenses, especially extended-wear soft lenses, generally last only a year or two. But their added comfort explains why approximately 80 percent of all contact lens wearers choose soft lenses.

The harder the lens, the longer it will take to adjust to it. And if you stop wearing hard lenses for a while, you might have to start getting adjusted to them all over again. Since there are times when you shouldn't wear your lenses—when you have an eye infection, a cold, or a black eye, for example—this can be an important consideration. If you do switch back to glasses for a while, your vision could be distorted by "spectacle blur," the result of your cornea having been temporarily molded into a new shape by the hard lens. The cornea, however, will eventually go back to its normal shape—probably just when you decide it's time to switch back to hard contact lenses again.

Gas-permeable lenses have some of the same problems, but to a much lesser degree. They are also more comfortable than hard lenses, are easier to adjust to, and cost about the same.

Soft lenses are the most comfortable. Because they are also bigger and cover more of the eye, they tend to stay in place more easily. And because they let in more oxygen, they can be worn for longer periods. If you do have to switch back to glasses for a while, that adjustment is also easier, because there is usually no spectacle blur.

Don't Wear Your Lenses If . . .

Colds, the flu, and allergies can make wearing contact lenses uncomfortable. Under such circumstances, the lenses could even damage your eyes. So if your lenses irritate your eyes when you're sick, don't wear them.

Also, if you're the sort of person who cries easily and you expect you're going to be crying—whether they be tears of laughter or of sadness—leave your lenses at home.

But some people, usually those with a moderate to large astigmatism, are just physically incapable of seeing as clearly through soft lenses as they are through hard lenses.

A person with an astigmatism has an eye that is not completely round. A hard or gas-permeable lens functions like a girdle to help shape the eye—making it more perfectly round. A soft lens, however, just drapes over the eye, like the soft piece of plastic that it is.

Soft lenses are also harder to take care of and require regular disinfection as well as cleaning.

It is important to remember that some people never adjust to contact lenses. You can insure yourself against wasting the price of lenses you'll never wear by finding one of the growing number of eye doctors who is willing to refund your money or exchange your contact lenses for a new pair of glasses if the lenses don't work out after a specified length of time.

Examining Contact Lens Options

As they say on Madison Avenue: Never try to sell someone plain, ordinary soap when you can sell them new, improved, plain, ordinary soap instead. Although there aren't as many features and secret ingredients that can be added to contact lenses as can be added to soap, stereo systems, or station wagons, the manufacturers are trying.

Bifocal Lenses

Because many people who wear contact lenses also need reading glasses, manufacturers have come up with bifocal contact lenses—two different kinds of them.

One type looks like a miniversion of a lens in a pair of bifocal eyeglasses. The normal vision portion is on top and the bifocal or reading vision portion is on the bottom. Even though the bottoms of the contact lenses are weighted to keep them in the right place, they rarely stay there. Every time the person wearing them blinks, the lenses shift—and only occasionally shift back into the proper position.

The second type of bifocal contact lens has the bifocal portion all around the rim, leaving the center portion for normal viewing. To see normally (distant vision), you have to look straight ahead, sort of like looking through the hole in an optical doughnut. You get the bifocal (near vision) effect by looking up, down, or off to one side. If you want to see something normally that's off to one side, you have to first turn your head to face it so you can look at it straight on. All in all, this type of lens is not yet one of the industry's crowning achievements, but improvements are on the way.

Another alternative for people who need bifocals is to wear two entirely different lenses. One lens gives one eye normal distance vision, and the other lens gives the other eye the strength it needs to read or do close work. The "dominant eye" is usually the one corrected for distance. The "nondominant" eye usually gets the reading lens.

To determine which of your eyes is the dominant one, either aim through a rifle sight or roll a piece of paper into a tube and look through it. The dominant eye is the one you automatically "sight" with.

As you can imagine, having each eye corrected for different degrees of vision can take more than a little getting used to. But more and more people are opting for that approach.

Tinted Lenses

Tinted lenses don't change what you see when you look out of your eyes, just what people see when they look into them. As the title of an old country-and-western song puts it: "Don't That Make Your Brown Eyes Blue."

Actually, the lenses usually aren't dark enough to totally change your eye color, but they will slightly alter or enhance whatever natural color is there. The tinted lenses use dyes, approved by the Food and Drug Administration, that will not harm your eyes.

By the way, most eye doctors recommend that you get your hard lenses tinted either light blue or light gray. This is done not for any cosmetic reason, but to make the lenses easier to locate when they are out of your eyes—in a sink full of water, on the pillow, or on the carpet, for example.

X-Chrom Lenses

As with so many other "new" discoveries, lenses to help color-blind people distinguish colors have been around for a lot longer than you might think—more than a century, in fact. It was back in 1857 that red and green filters were first mounted on spectacle frames to help red-green color-blind people distinguish between colors. Red-green color blindness is the most common form of the condition.

Today, people can use a single X-Chrom contact lens and get the same effect. The lens is red and is placed over one eye. By filtering out specific wavelengths of light in that one eye, it creates a contrast with what the other eye sees that helps the wearer differentiate between red and green objects. In one study, 33 of 40 red-green color-blind people given an X-Chrom lens reported a significant improvement in their ability to distinguish colors.

Bandage Lenses

Occasionally a contact lens is used as a "bandage" to help an injured cornea heal. The lens protects the cornea from the eyelid's blinking and from dust and other debris that might be blown into the eye.

Bandage lenses are usually clear; they have no correcting power. They are designed to help an eye heal, not to improve its vision. If you normally wear contact lenses, you will have to go back to your glasses while the bandage lens is in place.

Since these lenses are sometimes left in place for months at a time to give the cornea enough time to heal, deposits and infections can occur. People wearing bandage lenses need to have their eyes and lenses examined regularly.

Keratoconus Lenses

Keratoconus—from the Greek words *kera* ("cornea") and *kōnus* ("cone")—refers to a relatively common hereditary problem that causes a person's cornea to change from its normal round shape to a cone shape. Hard keratoconus contact lenses are used to correctively "round" the surface of such an eye in much the same way that hard contact lenses help "round" the eyes of people suffering from astigmatism.

Orthokeratotic Lenses

Orthokeratology is an expensive, time-consuming, and potentially dangerous process that doesn't work very well or very often. The procedure is performed by a small number of orthokeratologists, and it is designed to correct nearsightedness by flattening the cornea of the eye.

While a rigid contact lens will correct vision while it is being worn, orthokeratotic lenses are supposed to permanently reshape the eye.

The cornea of a nearsighted eye is often a little on the steep side. To correct this steepness, a patient is given a series of progressively flatter lenses every four to six weeks for a period of 18 to 30 months, until either the nearsightedness has been eliminated or the cornea is incapable of being bent any further out of shape.

Even after the eye has been reshaped, the patient must wear a "retainer" lens to hold it in shape. Orthokeratologists do claim, however, that patients can go without the lens for days or even weeks at a time.

Scientific studies contradict these claims. They show that the procedure is not predictable and that the amount of nearsightedness that can be corrected is very small.

Furthermore, the quality of the "corrected" vision is never stable, nor is it as good as could be achieved with glasses or conventional lenses. Many people who have undergone the process say their vision is distorted—as though they are looking at the world through a dirty windshield or a fish bowl.

Then there are the additional concerns about expense, time, and the constant pressure on the cornea that could lead to eye problems a lot more serious than nearsightedness.

Makeup Tips for Lens Wearers

Your contact lenses will automatically collect all sorts of pollutants. How you apply eye makeup and the type you use could add to the problem. Here are some tips.

- Wash your hands with a nonoily soap before handling your lenses. Then insert the lenses before you apply your makeup. Not only will you be better able to see what you are doing, but you will also eliminate the chance of makeup getting on your lenses while you're inserting them.
- Choose an eye makeup designed for contact lens wearers or for people with allergies.
- If you use a moisturizing cream around your eyes, use one formulated specifically for that area. Regular facial lotions are more fluid and more likely to run into your eyes.
- The more mascara there is on your eyelashes, the more mascara there is that can fall into your eyes.
- Close your eyes when applying powdered cosmetics.
- Use a sponge applicator instead of a brush. There will be less makeup flying away with a sponge, especially if you tap it a few times to remove any excess powder before applying it.
- Rubbing your eyes while you're wearing contact lenses is bad enough; doing it while wearing contact lenses *and* eye makeup is even worse.
- Be as careful when taking off your makeup as you are when putting it on.

CHAPTER 5

LENS MAKING
MORE THAN JUST
A GRIND

> Get thee glass eyes;
> And like a scurvy politician, seem
> To see things thou dost not.
>
> Shakespeare, *King Lear*

Both eyeglasses and glass eyes go back a lot further than you might think.

In 1268, the English scientist Roger Bacon wrote that people with weak eyes could read small print by reading through a piece of glass "shaped like the lesser segment of a sphere, with the convex [rounded] side toward the eye."

Although the advice was good, it could be ignored by the general population for the simple reason that the general population was illiterate. Even if they could read, books were so rare and so jealously guarded that the general public couldn't get their hands on them, let alone their eyes.

Nearly 200 years later, in the mid-1440s, a goldsmith in Mainz, Germany, named Johannes Gutenberg changed all that.

He and his partner, Johann Fust, took a new and somewhat radical idea called movable type and started the world's first publishing empire. A few decades later people who had been raised not knowing what a book was found themselves complaining that even though they now had plenty of books, they couldn't read the fine print in them.

Why did it take the invention of movable type and the creation of mass-produced books and pamphlets to spark the development of lenses? Think about it. There are very few things you need to stare at—for hours at a time—that are smaller than the print on this page.

All of a sudden, Roger Bacon's commentary about looking through "the lesser segment of a [glass] sphere" became more than just a curious bit of trivia. It became the cornerstone of a brand-new industry created to grind the lenses that all of those lately literate people with weak eyes and a new library needed to read their books.

A Guild for Glasses

Early magnifying lenses were held closer to what was being read than to the eye. It was just a matter of time, though, before someone realized that the lens would also work if you held it near the eye. Then someone figured out that you could use a different lens for each eye.

But the important part was the lens.

Many people knew just how important, and the lens-making industry grew to the point that in 1629, England's King Charles I gave a charter to the Worshipful Company of Spectaclemakers of London, which had formed "for the better order, rule and government of those using the Art and Mistry [sic] of Spectaclemaking."

According to the rules established by the Worshipful Company—also known as a guild—a person could become an apprentice at age 16. After nine years of work—years spent learning everything from grinding the lenses to making the frames—an apprentice could submit a sample of eyeglasses to the guild's examining board. If the glasses were good enough, the apprentice became a master and could open his or her own shop. It was one of the few guilds that allowed women members.

The emphasis then was on making spectacles that fit their wearers' heads, not their eyes. As far as the "prescription" was concerned, spectacles were sold according to age. It was assumed, for example, that all 30 year olds with eye trouble would have similar vision problems, and when one came in for glasses, the choice of lenses was limited to those deemed suitable for 30-year-old eyes. Sometimes the person who needed the glasses would order them by mail, asking only for a pair of glasses suitable for a specific age and size.

Over the years, the process of fitting glasses to individual visual needs developed along with the process of making them. Most of the developments and progress in the craft of lens making took place in Europe. So did the developments in lens using. Along with the best lenses came the best telescopes, cameras, and microscopes to use those lenses. In fact, the United States got nearly all of its optical glass from Europe until the outbreak of World War I. Once the war began and America decided to team up with England against the Germans—Europe's premier lens makers—American companies had to learn how to make their own.

The Art of Making Glass

The basic process of making glass is neither hard nor mysterious. The first glassmakers very possibly "discovered" their craft after watching what happens to a sand beach when lightning strikes it. The "hard ice" that formed out of the fused sand served as their inspiration. They then probably experimented with supplying their own heat and mixtures of sand and other components to first create colored ceramic glazes. Their craft eventually evolved into glassmaking. It is worth noting that the word *glaze* refers to both windows and to the coating put on pottery.

But just as there is a big difference between playing the guitar and playing it well, there is also a big difference between making window glass and making optical glass.

Today, optical glass is made by machines according to complicated and often secret formulas that call for the blending of special sands with minerals, chemicals, and even some rejected optical glass from other batches. These mixtures are cooked for more than a day in fire pots that have to be preheated for several days before even receiving the mixture.

The mixture is cooked until it turns into a liquid as thick as mud or molasses. It is then poured on a preheated iron table and rolled out to a specific thickness. After the mixture is rolled out, the table is moved—by conveyer belt—into another section of the oven, where it is slowly allowed to cool. It is still much too hot for anyone's hands to come close to it, let alone work on it.

One of the first lessons learned by glassblowers and anyone else who works with glass is that you can't tell how hot a piece of glass is by looking at it. Glass hot enough to give you a severe burn doesn't look any different from room-temperature glass.

Once the glass cools, automatic shears cut out individual pieces, which are pressed into lens blanks. Still traveling by conveyer belt, the blanks go on to another furnace, where they are cooked and cooled yet again.

Getting the glass to the right temperature is only part of the process. The glass has to be heated and cooled for a specific period of time, and when it is allowed to cool down, it must do so slowly. If molten glass is cooled too quickly, it becomes very brittle.

Once cooled, the individual lens blanks are then inspected, machine polished to meet the specific requirements for that batch of lenses, inspected yet again, and then shipped to the offices of the modern descendants of the Worshipful Company of Spectaclemakers and into the hands of the anxiously waiting master craftsmen employed therein.

Personalizing the Product

It's up to the optician to make sure that the lenses you need and want will fit into the frames you picked. But there is more involved than just cutting the lenses to fit the frames and popping them in. Each lens must have the right "strength" or prescription (see "How Lens Prescriptions Are Filled" on page 58).

And for the prescription to work as intended, the lens must be carefully positioned.

Alignment for Astigmatism

Lens placement is especially important to people with an astigmatism—people whose eyeballs are not perfectly round. Their glasses must compensate for this odd shape, so the entire curve of the lens must be both tuned to and turned to the curve of the eyeball.

How Lens Prescriptions Are Filled

Some 6-foot-tall men wear size 6 shoes, others wear size 16. The vast majority are somewhere in the middle.

In the same way that it would be impossible to come up with a one-size-fits-all shoe that would guarantee a perfect fit to every man in the world, it would be equally impossible to make a one-prescription-fits-all pair of glasses.

In fact, they can't even come up with a one-size-fits-all lens blank.

As you read earlier, it is the light-bending curvature of the lens that determines its power or prescription. Each lens has two curves, one on the front surface and one on the back surface. There are virtually millions of different possible combinations of curves.

To simplify matters, lens manufacturers generally make about six different blank lenses, each with a different "base curve." These blanks are made by the millions and sold to finishing labs, which then grind the front surface of each lens into a curve that will fit an individual prescription.

While most lens manufacturers make five or six different lens blanks, nearly all prescriptions can be made using a lens with one of the three common base curves. The other lens blanks are kept in stock for the same reason that shoe stores routinely carry size 13 shoes. Some people need them.

But what about a man who needs a size 15, or a size 3? Special lens blanks, like special shoes, can be ordered from custom manufacturers.

Imagine making a plaster cast of your feet and then stand-ing in the wet plaster until it dries so that the cast matches your footprint like a second skin. Imagine standing in that cast and sensing how smooth it feels. Now imagine turning around and standing in it with your feet facing the opposite way. The cast still fits the contours of your feet, but it doesn't fit the way you have your feet in them.

It's pretty much the same with an astigmatism. The lens has to be precisely positioned in the frame to fit the irregular curva-ture of the eye. The optical "top" of the lens must be at the op-tical "top" of the glasses.

Bifocals and Trifocals

The process is a bit more complicated for people with bifo-cals—glasses with two prescriptions on each lens. Bifocal wear-ers usually look through the top portion of the glasses for gen-eral walking around and "seeing" and through the bottom portion for reading.

While some bifocal lenses are made from two different pieces of glass fused together, others are made out of one piece that has been ground into two separate prescriptions.

The whole process is taken a step further with trifocals. Each lens of these glasses has three separate prescriptions.

The most common type of trifocal has a general "seeing" lens on top, a "reading" lens on the bottom, and a "middle dis-tance" lens in—you guessed it—the middle.

Some people, however, have trifocals made with the general "seeing" lens in the middle and "reading" lenses at the bottom and at the top. This type of lens would be handy for a person who has to read things above his head as well as below. A piano player, for example, might need this type of lens so he could read the music on the music stand by glancing up from "read-ing" the keys.

Many people dislike wearing bifocals—and trifocals—if there is a clear and distinct line between the different pieces of lens. They feel that just being seen in bifocals makes them look old. They also complain about the "jump" in vision as their eye travels from one lens to the other.

Off-the-Rack Reading Glasses

Those of you who have never worn glasses have a rude awakening ahead at around age 42 (give or take a few years). You may find that you suddenly (or gradually) have trouble reading fine print—the sort found in a telephone directory—or that you have to hold reading material farther away than normal to see it clearly.

Some people say that their arms have grown too short.

If this already sounds familiar, you have presbyopia, a condition in which we lose our ability to change the shape and, therefore, the focusing power of the lens inside our eye (see chapter 3).

A simple solution is reading glasses, also known as magnifying glasses. You've probably seen them in the drugstore, on the rotating racks. They cost about $10 to $15 a pair. Even many people who wear contact lenses may wear magnifying glasses over them for reading.

Magnifying glasses are numbered according to their magnifying power. The numbers generally run from + 1.00 to + 3.00, and increase in increments of 0.25. Both lenses will be the same power.

The racks usually have directions printed on them to help you pick the right pair of glasses. The directions tell you to start out with the + 1.00 or + 1.25 power, stand about 14 inches away from the rack and read the printing on it. If you have trouble, try glasses with more power.

You may need to boost the power slightly (+ 0.25 or + 0.50) every year or two as more focusing ability is lost.

You can obtain the same lens power in prescription glasses, of course, and the frames may be a lot more stylish and fit better. They will also be more expensive.

If you started out nearsighted, farsighted, or with a fair amount of astigmatism, you probably need prescription reading glasses, bifocals, or trifocals. But many people find the drugstore glasses very adequate.

People considering store-bought magnifying lenses typically have two questions. "Are the lenses of inferior quality?" and "Will I hurt my eyes if I pull too strong or too weak a prescription off the shelf?" The answer to both questions is no.

Some bifocals are made without that line. The two prescriptions blend together in a seamless piece of glass. While this hides the dreaded "bifocal line," it does create an area between the two lenses where vision is distorted, since the "blended" area fits neither the prescription for seeing nor the one for reading.

Plastic Lenses

No matter what prescription you need, you can probably get it in either glass or plastic. The choice is up to you.

Plastic is lighter, easier to work with, less likely to fog, and more resistant to shattering. The strongest lenses available today are made from polycarbonate, the plastic used to make bullet-proof windows. Polycarbonate lenses can be coated, tinted, and ground to any prescription. They weigh about half as much as glass lenses (for a detailed look at safety lenses, turn to chapter 3).

The light weight of plastic is a major bonus, especially if you are required to wear the thicker sort of glasses that your more tactless acquaintances might refer to as "Coke bottle lenses." There are some drawbacks, however. Plastic lenses are more expensive to make and are more likely to scratch.

Plastic lenses also need special care. While you can clean a glass lens with any piece of soft cloth, plastic lenses should be washed with soap and water and wiped clean while they are still wet. If you wipe them while they are dry, you will generate a static electricity field on the lenses. This static charge will attract dust and dirt that will get the lenses dirty again that much more quickly.

Tints, Coatings, and Other Options

Some lenses—both glass and plastic—are *colored* as they are made by adding dye to the lens mixture. This can be a problem, though, for people with thick lenses or lens sections, because the color darkens as thickness increases.

Polarized lenses are made by adding chemicals to the glass or plastic when they are being made. Sometimes polarized plastic is laminated to a glass lens.

Polarized lenses reduce glare from water, snow, car windows, and other reflective surfaces by allowing only light coming in at specific angles to pass through. That is why tilting your head or turning polarized lenses changes the amount of visible light.

Other lenses are *coated* after they are made. There are five types of lens coatings: dielectric, color, nonreflective, scratch resistant, and mirror.

- A dielectric coating is used to block out both UV and infrared radiation.
- Color coating a lens does just what the words imply.
- A nonreflective coating can be applied to the back of the lens, the side closest to the eye. When light strikes the lens from the back—from behind the person wearing them—the light passes out through the front of the lens and is not reflected back into the eyes.
- A good scratch-resistant coating can make a pair of plastic lenses almost as scratch resistant as glass ones. A scratch-resistant coating could also be applied over other coatings to prevent them from being scratched or rubbing off the lens.
- A mirror coating prevents a great deal of light from getting through the lens and turns a pair of glasses into a one-way mirror. No one can see in, and the person looking out through them is protected from infrared radiation. Mirrored lenses are actually the coolest lenses to wear—in terms of heat, not style—and should be worn outdoors in intense glare from either direct sunlight or sunlight reflected from ice, water, or snow.

Photochromic lenses also block out sunlight, but without the use of any coating. Sometimes referred to as photosensitive or sun-sensitive lenses, these "automatic sunglasses" darken when exposed to bright light. When the light decreases, the lenses lighten up again.

It is not the brightness of the light that makes them darken, however; it's the UV light that is part of normal sunlight. They stay dark as long as they are exposed to ultraviolet light.

Many people wear photochromic lenses instead of sunglasses. But if you are going to be outdoors in the bright sunlight a great deal, you might want to get a regular pair of sunglasses as well. The latter will block out more light and do so as soon as you put them on.

Other drawbacks of photochromic lenses are that they tend to get darker in cold weather than they do in hot weather, and they can't reach full darkness while you are driving because the windshield blocks some of the UV rays needed to trigger the darkening process.

These lenses also take time to lighten up. Entering a dark room from bright sunlight could be a problem until both your eyes and the lenses adjust. And they never go completely clear; they always have a slight tint to them. This could be a problem for older adults who usually require more light in order to see.

Frames

No matter which type of lens you pick, you will also have to choose the frames to put them in.

Frames are usually made out of metal or plastic and come in innumerable sizes, styles, and colors. Some even have sequins.

If you are indecisive, there are numerous fashion consultants—some trained and some self-appointed—who can tell you which type of frame is "in" and which type is "out"; which frames are right for your face, your hair, or your occupation; what colors bring out your best features or match your teeth . . . whatever. Some of these fashion consultants might even know what they're doing.

In terms of style and color, get the glasses you like. It's perfectly natural to ask people their opinions, but the final choice is yours. While you aren't going to be looking at yourself wearing them, you are the one who will be wearing them. If you get talked into frames that you dislike, they'll spend more time in their case than on your nose, and the glasses won't do you any good.

Whatever style you choose, they should be sturdy and well constructed with smoothly working hinges and screw joints.

Your glasses should fit lightly on the ears, nose, and temples, so that you're hardly aware that you are wearing them. But while they should be light, they must also be snug. They won't do your eyes or your checking account any good if they keep falling off your face.

They should also be suitable for what you're going to be doing while you are wearing them. A pair of eyeglasses for a person who spends most of his time at a desk might be different from those needed by someone who wears them while climbing mountains, playing basketball, riding bucking broncos, or looking through a telescope.

By the way, when your glasses are not on your nose, they belong in their case. That's why your optician gave you one. With eyeglasses routinely costing more than $100 a pair, keeping them unprotected in your purse, pocket, or pack is an invitation to an expensive accident. Most eyeglasses that are broken meet that fate when they are not being worn rather than when they are.

So much for choosing the right frame material, color, and style, and how to keep your glasses safe. Before any style choices can be made, you first have to determine which size you need.

The size frame you need depends on the size of your head and the distance between your eyes. An optician will determine your P.D. (pupillary distance) by measuring the distance between the pupils of both eyes. That measurement is important because the optical center of each lens should be right in front of the pupil. The farther apart your eyes are, the farther apart the optical centers of the lenses must be.

People with large heads and eyes that are relatively far apart usually need larger lenses and larger frames. And as with so many other things in life, not all styles are available in all sizes.

The final considerations that need to be mentioned are the weight and thickness of the lenses. Thick and heavy lenses need frames that are sturdy enough to support them.

How Contact Lenses Are Made

If you wear contact lenses, you can avoid having to make most of the decisions that selecting a pair of glasses requires. Your eyes themselves serve as contact lens frames, so there are no questions of style to worry about, and unless you buy tinted contact lenses, your tears—or eyedrops—will usually provide the lenses with all the coatings they might need.

But while contact lenses are designed to be simple to wear, making them isn't easy. No matter which of three different manufacturing processes is used, exact measurements and standards must be met for each individual lens.

Lathe-Cut Lenses

The lenses start out as hard plastic "buttons." The buttons are made out of different materials following different formulas, according to the type of lens being made and the company making them. The buttons are cut on a computer-controlled lathe and then smoothed and buffed.

Both hard and soft lenses can be made this way, because a soft lens is hard while it is being made. Once made, a soft lens is chemically treated—"hydrated"—to be turned into a soft lens.

Molded Lenses

As the name implies, molded lenses are made from a mold. Both soft and hard lenses can be made this way.

The molds are usually made of either glass or plastic and are actually hand-formed lenses that can be used again and again.

Liquid plastic is poured into the mold under pressure and then allowed to set. Once the plastic dries, the lenses are removed and later polished.

Spin-Cast Lenses

Spin casting is another method used to create soft lenses. A mold is created, but instead of pouring liquid plastic into the mold under pressure—as is done with conventionally molded lenses—a computer control is used to make sure that just the right amount of liquid is "spurted" into the mold.

Computers also are used to spin the mold at just the right speed to make sure that the plastic "coats" the inside of the mold. When it dries, the lens is peeled off the mold. This method produces lenses that are so smooth that they don't even need to be polished.

Roger Bacon would be amazed.

CHAPTER 6

IRRITATIONS AND INFECTIONS GETTING THE RED OUT

My eyes are red.
Paul Newman's are blue.
I'd rather have
Paul Newman's eyes.
Wouldn't you?

People with brown eyes might wish they had green eyes, while those with green may yearn for blue—but nobody wants red eyes. Even pink eyes are enough to send people to the doctor. In fact, conjunctivitis—the clinical term for both red eye and pinkeye—is one of the most common problems an eye doctor sees.

Conjunctivitis can be caused by irritants, trauma, infections, medications, even the common cold. Rubbing the eyes or swimming in chlorinated pools may cause a mild and temporary case of the condition, as can wind, sand, and dust. Often the cure for a mild case of conjunctivitis is time. Once the irritant is removed, the condition clears.

Other causes and cases can be much more serious and may

even lead to blindness. Often the only one who can tell you which type you have is a doctor, because the initial symptoms are very similar.

In each case the underlying source of the redness is the same. The conjunctiva, an almost transparent, thin membrane that covers the white of the eye, is filled with tiny blood vessels that bring nutrients, protective antibodies, and other substances to the surface of the eye. Whenever the conjunctiva is irritated, these blood vessels become dilated—they fill up with blood. These widened blood vessels are what makes the eye look pink or red.

Now let's take a closer look at some of the causes of the red eye and other irritating eye problems.

Drops for Bloodshot Eyes

Most nonprescription eyedrops are vasoconstrictors. They "get the red out" by constricting, or shrinking, the blood vessels in your eyes. Some of these drops also contain an antihistamine that relieves the itchiness that often accompanies eye irritations.

The effect of these drops usually lasts for a few hours. When they wear off, sometimes the redness comes back worse than ever (the "rebound" phenomenon). If your eyes continue to be bloodshot or there is an excessive amount of discharge, you may have an eye infection or some other problem that requires a doctor's attention.

Over-the-counter eyedrops also carry warnings about avoiding excessive use. Heed them. Using them too frequently can cause more eye problems than they can cure.

Blepharitis

Quite often, a red eye doesn't indicate a problem in the eye itself but rather in the eyelid. Blepharitis is an inflammation of the eyelid margins and the eyelids and meibomian glands, the oil-producing glands in the lids.

One of the most common eye problems, blepharitis causes

discharge from the eyes that can make your eyelids stick shut when you wake up in the morning. Your eyelashes may be crusty, turn white, and even fall out. Occasionally the cornea can be damaged by the bacteria or toxins that come in contact with the eye from the inflamed eyelid.

Blepharitis is a chronic problem for many people, and while it may not always be curable, it can be kept under control.

There are numerous causes, including infections, seborrhea, excessive rubbing of the eyes, and allergies to drugs or cosmetics. Blepharitis can even be a side effect of measles, scarlet fever, and other diseases.

The most common cause is a low-grade *Staphylococcus* infection of the rims of the eyelids. The staph bacteria like the oily, scaly environment of the lid margins, and they thrive there. It may be the toxin produced by the bacteria that gets into the eyes and makes them red.

No matter what causes blepharitis, the treatment usually consists of cleansing the eyelid margins and lashes with a baby shampoo solution applied with a cotton-tipped swab or washcloth.

Next, the oily secretions in the glands have to be removed. To get them out, first apply a hot compress over your closed eyes for 10 minutes or so. Then massage the eyelids, using a gentle rubbing action. Massage the upper eyelid downward to work the oil secretion out of the glands in much the same way you squeeze toothpaste out of a tube. Then massage the lower lid upward.

As a rule, this eyelid treatment must be performed every night for at least a week or two until the problem is under control. But since blepharitis can be a chronic condition that will come back once treatment is halted, you might have to do it once or twice a week—for the rest of your life. While this is not a pleasant prospect, most people who have the condition make it a part of their daily ritual, like brushing their teeth.

It is a good idea for the doctor to take a culture of the secretion before the treatment starts. If he can identify a specific type of bacteria, he can prescribe either an antibiotic you can take orally or an antibiotic ointment to be rubbed into the eyelids. But this ointment won't work very well unless you keep the eyelids clean.

Lid Twitches, Tics, and Spasms

Eyelids can present other annoying problems besides inflammation. Involuntary movements or spasms, for example, come in three basic varieties.

Tics and twitches. No one really knows what causes minor eyelid tics and twitches. They are usually associated with being tired or under a great deal of stress, or needing glasses.

Essential blepharospasm. This is a rare condition in which both eyes close involuntarily. In advanced cases, the neck and mouth might also twitch when the spasms strike. No one knows what causes the spasms, which can be troublesome and incapacitating. Although biofeedback and drugs are occasionally successful, surgery may be required to cure the problem. Recently, botulinum toxin, derived from the bacteria that cause botulism food poisoning, has been injected into the muscles undergoing spasm with good results.

Hemifacial spasm. This is a spasm that affects the eyelid muscles—and sometimes the muscles around the mouth—on one side of the face. It is caused by an artery pressing against the nerve of the facial muscles. Surgery is usually required to relieve the pressure, but sometimes medication will do the job.

Sties and Similar Problems

Even though each of these three different types of eyelid infection has a specific definition and produces a different type of lump, the words *hordeolum, sty,* and *chalazion* are frequently used somewhat interchangeably. We often lump these lumps together and call them chalazia.

If you have a hordeolum, a red, swollen, and tender area develops in one of the lids because of a boil or abscess in the affected gland. When the meibomian gland is the one affected, it is known as an internal hordeolum. When one of the smaller glands is infected, it is known as a sty.

A chalazion is a similar type of inflammation affecting the meibomian glands. The eyelid becomes swollen and tender, and a nodule develops inside the lid. While the condition often goes away as mysteriously and quickly as it develops, it can become a cosmetic problem or even distort your vision. It should be treated with hot compresses as soon as it is detected.

Apply a hot compress for 15 minutes four times a day. If the swelling has not been reduced after a week or two, the abscess might have to be drained by your doctor.

The draining is a simple, in-office procedure. The doctor will anesthetize the eyelid and make a small cut in the back side of the lid so the pus can drain. Then he will apply an antibiotic ointment, and he may even place a patch on the eye after the procedure.

For reasons still unknown, some people are plagued with these problems over and over again. There is no way to prevent them, but scrubbing the eyelid margins with baby shampoo on a regular basis does seem to reduce their frequency.

Adenovirus

Once called shipyard eye because it was first isolated and identified in a California shipyard during World War II, adenovirus is a common but relatively harmless eye infection that can hit with epidemic proportions and sweep through schools, hospitals, doctors' offices, factories, and even entire communities. Summertime epidemics of the malady are often referred to as swimming pool conjunctivitis or pinkeye.

With adenovirus infections, the eye becomes very red and swollen. There may be some discharge and sensitivity to light. You can usually find a swollen gland on the side of the head, just in front of the ear.

Fortunately, adenovirus does not usually require any medication, nor does any medication knock out the virus. Like the common cold, it will cure itself. But as with a cold, even though you cannot cure it, you can make yourself more comfortable while you have it. Warm compresses not only feel good, they give you a chance to close your eyes, relax, and lie down.

Like a cold, adenovirus is very contagious, but following a few simple safety steps will help limit its spread. You should wash your hands after touching the infected eye, and towels and washcloths used by the infected person should be kept separate from the rest of the family's linens—at least until they've been washed.

Even newspapers, silverware, or a handshake could be a way of transmitting the virus to another person, if that person touches the infected material and then touches his eye. Remember also, that if one eye is infected and the other is not, don't touch one eye and then the other. Most cases do ultimately affect both eyes, but a little caution could help keep the infection rate down.

A similar type of infection, known as acute hemorrhagic conjunctivitis, spread throughout the entire world in 1969, at the same time as the *Apollo 11* mission to the moon. Because some people were convinced that the virus was brought back by the spacecraft, the malady was dubbed *Apollo 11* conjunctivitis.

There are two principal differences between it and adenovirus. First, acute hemorrhagic conjunctivitis is even more contagious than adenovirus. Second, the eyes become even redder because of tiny hemorrhages from blood vessels within the conjunctiva itself. Like adenovirus, "space conjunctivitis"—as some people still call it, cures itself and often does so much more quickly than adenovirus.

Gonorrheal Conjunctivitis

Bacteria can also frequently cause conjunctivitis. One of the most serious is the bacterium that causes gonorrhea. If this bacterium gets in the eye, it produces a type of conjunctivitis that features a great deal of redness, swelling, and pus. Gonorrheal conjunctivitis is a medical emergency and requires immediate treatment, usually with penicillin.

Trachoma

Caused by a bacteria-like agent called *Chlamydia*, trachoma is the leading cause of blindness in the world today. In fact, it's been one of the leading causes of blindness since history began. One of the oldest diseases known to humanity, it was first recognized in the twenty-seventh century B.C.

Although it is now quite rare in the United States, trachoma used to be common among American Indians. Currently it is quite common in Africa, South America, and Asia, affecting more than 400 million people worldwide. The disease is found primarily in less-developed countries, where it may be transferred by flies. It can also be transmitted by community towels or other items shared by large numbers of people. But the disease does tend to disappear as economic and hygienic conditions improve.

As the infection develops, the conjunctiva becomes inflamed, leading to scarring. This causes the eyelashes to turn in and irritate the cornea, which in turn can lead to a blinding corneal infection.

Trachoma is a major health problem and the target of some of the most concentrated efforts in eye research. Fortunately, the disease responds well to antibiotic treatment. The problem in the field, however, is often a lack of cooperation and transportation. Sometimes available medicine never reaches the people who need it. Another problem, especially in some of the more remote parts of the world, is educating people about how to avoid reinfection.

There is, by the way, a slightly different strain of chlamydia that causes nonspecific urethritis, the most common type of venereal disease. This infection can occasionally be transferred to the eye.

Eye Infections in Newborns

Ophthalmia neonatorum is a form of conjunctivitis that can hit newborn infants when the mother has a genital infection such as herpes, gonorrhea, or chlamydia. The infection reaches the baby as it passes through the birth canal.

To protect the baby's eyes, a 1 percent silver nitrate solution or an antibiotic ointment is put into the baby's eyes at birth.

This preventive treatment is required by law in 47 states and the District of Columbia. In the remaining three states, it is required only in births attended by midwives or in cases in which the presence of disease is suspected.

In ten states, the requirement may be waived if the parents object—and lots of parents object. (After all, they reason, neither of them is the sort of person who would have that sort of disease.) If the parents object, and there is a genital infection, the baby can develop a serious eye infection.

Herpes

A serious case of the red eye or conjunctivitis can also stem from the herpes simplex virus. This is the same virus that produces cold sores or fever blisters, and a close relative of the virus that causes genital herpes.

If you have had one herpes-related eye infection, you may get another one, and another one. They tend to recur because the virus resides in the nerves around the eye and periodically travels down those nerves to cause trouble. More than half the population of the United States has the virus, but for reasons still unknown, it causes problems for only a small percentage of us.

One thing that we do know for sure is that the active infection can be triggered by stress, fever, or intense sunlight. Sometimes, avoiding these triggers can help prevent another attack.

When herpes does strike the eye, it can cause more than just conjunctivitis. It can also hit the cornea and cause major problems. When the virus is multiplying, it produces tiny clusters of ulcers—called dendrites—that branch out over the surface of the eye. Like the corneal infections that accompany adenovirus, dendrites will usually disappear on their own as the immune system mounts an attack on the virus. Treating them with antiviral eye drops will often speed their disappearance.

The real problems begin when the virus gets into the deeper corneal tissues and causes the sort of severe inflammation that can lead to blurred vision, pain, and corneal scarring—permanent scarring. If permanent damage happens, a corneal transplant may be required. Sometimes, too, the virus can go even deeper and infect the iris or the retina.

Steroid or cortisone-type eyedrops can be used to treat this deeper form of corneal herpes, but sometimes the medication can make it even worse. While steroids do suppress inflammation, they also suppress the immune system's ability to get rid of the virus that started the trouble in the first place. As a rule, it's usually better to avoid steroid eyedrops whenever possible.

Still another herpes virus, the varicella-zoster virus, causes chicken pox and shingles. If the shingles are around an eye, they can cause a red eye and serious inflammation inside the eye itself. This type of infection usually is accompanied by skin vesicles—small fluid-filled bumps—around the eye and intense pain in the forehead and scalp.

The virus travels along nerve fibers. But while these fibers have pathways throughout the skin, only one side of the body is affected. The nerves on the right side of the body do not connect with those on the left side. As a result, a shingles infection on one side of the face—as a rule—will not usually spread to the other.

The varicella-zoster virus can be devastating and requires prompt treatment. But even with prompt treatment, permanent eye damage cannot always be avoided.

We are now in an era when medications are being developed against viral infections in the same way that antibiotics have been developed against bacterial infections. An oral antiviral drug known as acyclovir (Zovirax), when taken early, will usually lead to a milder case of shingles than one would expect. But all herpes infections of the eye require careful monitoring by an ophthalmologist. One or more medications may be required, and it is important to be able to determine just when to increase or decrease the dosage of one or the other.

There is a great deal of time and effort being invested in developing a vaccine and drugs that work against the herpes virus. If you are at risk of developing a herpes virus eye infection, there are two things you can do until that vaccine is developed and perfected: Learn how to spot the early warning signs of a viral infection and avoid the triggers that can kick off a viral eye infection—too much sunlight, stress, or a fever.

Subconjunctival Hemorrhage

Did you ever wake up to find out that someone had apparently painted your eyeball bright red while you slept? Either the entire eye or just a spot on it? Don't bother looking for the paintbrush. The real cause was probably a subconjunctival hemorrhage.

Subconjunctival hemorrhages are caused by the rupture of tiny blood vessels within the conjunctiva. Sometimes you can actually pinpoint the trigger: a coughing or sneezing fit, vomiting, or straining during a bowel movement. Quite often, however, all you'll have is a red eye and not even a clue as to what caused the spontaneous breaking of a small blood vessel.

Whether you know the cause or not makes little difference. There is nothing you can do about it except wait for it to clear up on its own. That usually takes a week or two.

Dacryocystitis

Dacryocystitis is an infection of the lacrimal sac, more commonly called the tear duct.

When it occurs in infants, it is usually because the nasolacrimal duct in the nasal passage—which allows tears to drain from the inner corner of the eye to the inside of the nose—failed to open before birth. Eye infections can then easily develop in the closed duct, causing a noticeable swelling between the baby's eye and the bridge of the nose. Warm compresses, vigorous massage, and antibiotics are usually necessary to open the closed duct. If that fails, an ophthalmologist must use a thin probe to open it.

When dacryocystitis occurs in an adult, the cause is not always as clear-cut. It may be the aftereffect of an injury such as a broken nose, or a sinus infection may have closed off the nasal opening of the duct.

As with infants, the treatment for adults consists of warm compresses, massaging, and antibiotics. While an infant's nasolacrimal duct may be probed to open it when all else fails, an adult with the same problem may have to undergo a surgical procedure called a dacryocystorhinostomy. The operation forms a connection between the lacrimal sac and the nose.

Uveitis

Technically speaking, *uvea* is the collective term for the three different elements that form the pigmented tissue of the eye: the iris, ciliary body, and choroid. These tissues are joined together throughout the eye, and together they are known as the uveal tract.

Uveitis is the general name given to any inflammation that strikes the uvea. Such an inflammation can be blinding. While it normally strikes young adults or middle-aged people, it can happen at any time in life.

While uveitis is a general term, there are more specific ones. An inflammation that strikes the iris is called iritis. When it hits the ciliary body it is cyclitis. If the choroid is targeted, the result is choroiditis.

If the inflammation hits two areas, the names are combined. Iridocyclitis, for example, is an inflammation of the iris and the ciliary body, and chorioretinitis is an inflammation of the choroid and retina. If the entire eye is inflamed, it is called panuveitis.

There are numerous causes for the different types of uveitis. They include injuries; infections such as tuberculosis, herpes, and syphilis; illnesses such as chronic intestinal diseases and juvenile rheumatoid arthritis as well as other forms of arthritis; and problems with the immune system that cause the body to attack its own healthy tissues.

There is one common form of uveitis that mothers pass on to their unborn babies. It is caused by a parasite called toxoplasma that is found in cat feces. A pregnant woman can pick up the parasite by cleaning out a cat's litter box or by coming in contact with contaminated soil. The infection is then passed to the fetus.

When examining patients with uveitis, doctors usually look for a disease in another part of the body—such as an infection or arthritis—to determine if the eye inflammation is a side effect. Sometimes uveitis is the first—and occasionally the only—indication that something else is wrong. Treating the primary disease may lead to an improvement of the eye problem. Then again, it may not. In any event, doctors normally run a series of laboratory tests and take x-rays to rule out any contributing factor in patients with uveitis.

The symptoms of uveitis can include blurry vision, red eyes, photophobia (sensitivity to light), floating spots, and pain or an aching feeling around the eyes. Not everyone suffers all the symptoms, and some patients suffer no symptoms at all during the early stages.

Children with juvenile rheumatoid arthritis are in the high-risk category for uveitis. They are also among those victims very likely not to show any obvious symptoms of uveitis in the early stages. They should have their eyes checked on a regular basis.

As with other diseases, the earlier uveitis is spotted and treated, the better the chances are for a full recovery with no permanent loss of vision. Untreated uveitis can lead to a large number of even more serious eye problems such as cataracts, glaucoma, and damage to the retina, cornea, and optic nerve. Even though some forms of uveitis cannot be cured, prompt treatment can prevent further damage.

The most common treatments for uveitis involve antibiotics and other drugs that suppress inflammation, such as cortisone and anti-cancer drugs. Sometimes the doctor will dilate the pupil of the affected eye, or eyes, during this treatment. While this may temporarily blur vision, it also reduces pain and lessens the chances of further damage.

Scleritis

Like uveitis, scleritis is an inflammation. But as its name suggests, scleritis hits the sclera, the white part of the eye. It is accompanied by a deep, throbbing pain and redness.

A person may develop scleritis by itself, but it may also be a side effect of other conditions, such as rheumatoid arthritis. Scleritis is usually treated with anti-inflammatory drugs, either eyedrops or medication that can be swallowed. If untreated it can lead to thinning—or even perforation—of the sclera.

Keratitis

When the cornea is inflamed, it's called keratitis. It's also called a serious problem. Keratitis is a leading cause of blindness throughout the world.

The symptoms can include any or all of the following: a loss of sharpness of vision, redness, watery eyes, and a feeling that there's something in your eyes even when you know there isn't.

One of the most common forms of keratitis is caused by the herpes simplex virus, the same one that causes cold sores around your mouth. One of the simplest ways to give yourself herpes keratitis is to rub your eyes right after scratching a cold sore.

Another common cause of keratitis is contact lenses. If you wear contact lenses and develop any sort of eye problem, stop wearing them until you can check with your doctor. Keratitis is usually treated with medicated eyedrops.

Using Eyedrops Correctly

There are two problems with using any sort of eyedrops: getting them into the eye and getting them to stay in the eye long enough to do you some good.

Both problems are easy to solve—once you know how. And learning how is also easy, if you're willing to practice.

Since nonprescription eyedrops are not very expensive, you might want to buy a bottle and practice using them properly when there isn't an emergency. That way, you'll be ready to handle a real problem if it arises.

First let's practice getting the drops in the eye. The process is simple when you follow these steps.

1. Either lie down or sit down with your head tilted back and hold the open squeeze bottle a few inches above your eye. Use your other hand to pull the lower eyelid down so you don't blink when—or just before—the drops hit your eye.
2. Squeeze a drop or two inside your lower eyelid.
3. Close your eyes.

Now that you have the drops in your eye, you have to keep them there. The natural reaction is to open the eye as soon as the drops are in. But that lets the drops drain away before they can do your eye any good. Try one of these two techniques instead.

- Keep your eyes closed for 2 minutes.
- Place your finger at the point where the upper and lower eyelid meet near the nose and hold it there for a few minutes. Try not to blink. This blocks the passageway to the tear drainage ducts leading to the nose. It also allows drops to penetrate into the eye and prevents them from getting into the bloodstream.

Endophthalmitis

Endophthalmitis is a devasting but rare type of infection that can develop inside the eye after a serious eye injury or eye operation. Sometimes, however, it will develop for no known reason.

Endophthalmitis is a medical emergency that must be diagnosed and treated rapidly. An infection inside the eye can destroy the delicate retinal tissue within a matter of hours. When it does occur, the doctor must take a culture from the fluid inside the eye to identify the infecting microbe. Then an appropriate antibiotic must be administered for several days. The antibiotic may be given as eyedrops or intravenously. Sometimes it must be injected directly into the eye. It may sound like a drastic measure, but it's not nearly as drastic as blindness.

Fortunately endophthalmitis is a rare condition.

Yellow Eyes (Jaundice)

If the whites of your eyes are turning into the yellows, you probably have jaundice. That usually means a liver disease.

The yellow tint to your eyes—and to the rest of your body—is produced by excess production of a red-yellow pigment called bilirubin. When your liver is working properly, bilirubin is safely gotten rid of.

Jaundice can be the result of a number of different conditions, including all types of hepatitis, cirrhosis of the liver, a bile duct blockage, and certain types of anemia. Some medications can also trigger it. The only way you can get the yellow out of your eyes permanently is to get the problem causing the jaundice out of your body.

Graves' Disease

Graves' disease, also known as thyroid eye disease, isn't really an eye disease at all. It's an eye *socket* disease that affects the eyes.

It starts in the eye socket, or orbit—the bony cavity that

holds the eye. The tissue inside the socket becomes enlarged, forcing the eyes to move over to make room. As an added complication, the muscles that move the eyes can become swollen and may not function properly.

With some people, the eyes are thrown out of alignment by the increased pressure. This can cause crossed eyes and double vision. For others, the eyes are just pushed out a bit farther, giving the patient protruding eyes and a very wide-eyed or "pop-eyed" look. While many people consider this condition to be a disfigurement, a number of actors and actresses, such as Marty Feldman, Eddie Cantor, Peter Lorre, and Bette Davis, managed to use their bulging (exophthalmic) eyes to help develop and enhance their acting and comedic skills.

People with bulging eyes sometimes also develop abnormally large eyelid openings. This means that the eyelid has more eye to clean, bathe, and cover when it blinks.

Sometimes there is a part of the eye just below center—the

The Medication Dilemma

A dilemma is a situation in which the right answer to a question can also be the wrong one. Take, for example, medication.

Sometimes medication is the patient's best friend. Other times it's the worst enemy. And often neither you nor your doctor will know which it will be in your case until it's been tried.

Doctors prescribe eyedrops to clear up eye problems, but sometimes they can make matters worse. Most eyedrops are meant to be used for brief periods. When they are used for weeks or months, allergies or toxicity can develop. But sometimes that new problem is seen as a continuation or worsening of the original problem the eyedrops were meant to cure instead of a new problem caused by the medication itself. So the medication may be continued—or even increased—in a vain attempt to clear up the problem.

That's why it is so important to reevaluate treatment periodically. After all, if you're faced with a question to which the right answer might also be the wrong answer, sometimes the best thing you can do is ask a different question.

exposure region—that the eyelids just can't cover. This can cause the cornea to become dry and lead to eventual scarring and vision loss.

Regardless of how Graves' disease makes a person's eyes look, the condition can also cause increased pressure in the eyes themselves, which in turn can damage the optic nerve.

Graves' disease can hit one or both eyes and can affect each eye to a different degree. It also tends to hit women more than men.

Most—but not all—people who develop the condition have a history of an overactive thyroid gland. Graves' disease can develop years after the thyroid condition has been treated and taken care of. Why? No one knows.

We also don't know why it often lasts a year or two and then disappears—returning the eyes to their normal condition and position. Some people respond well to medication. Some don't. Others are cured without the benefit of any treatment whatsoever.

The main complaint of some people with the condition is swollen eyelids. One way to help this is to elevate the head of the bed about 6 inches. This puts gravity to work reducing the accumulation of fluid in the eyelids during the night.

For the self-conscious person with slightly protruding eyes, lightly tinted glasses will make it harder for people to notice the problem. If you already wear eyeglasses, you can have another pair made with a light tint added. If you don't need prescription glasses, you can get a pair of tinted lenses without any prescription at all.

If the eyes protrude so much that the cornea is becoming dry, you can use a soothing ophthalmic ointment at night and "artificial tears" during the day (for more information about artificial tears, see the "Dry Eyes" section on page 83).

In cases where a great deal of the cornea is being exposed, a surgeon might put a stitch or two at the corners of the eyelids to prevent the eyes from opening all the way. This is usually a temporary measure to prevent damage to the cornea.

In extreme cases where a person's sight is at stake, cortisone tablets are prescribed to reduce the pressure on the optic nerve and other vital ocular structures. A surgeon might also have to remove some of the bony wall lining the eye socket to give the swollen tissue a place to safely expand until the swelling can be brought under control. When this procedure is performed, the bony areas below the eyes—toward the nose—are usually the ones chipped away so that the swollen tissue can expand into the sinus cavities. Radiation therapy is sometimes used instead of surgery, but the results are usually slower and less predictable.

Some surgery might be required even after the condition is cured. If the eye muscles have been thrown permanently out of alignment by the disease, they might have to be realigned to uncross the eyes or correct double vision. Surgery might also have to be performed on the eyelids to remove excess skin or tissue or readjust their height.

No matter what treatment—if any—is needed to correct the eye problems stemming from thyroid eye disease, the patient's thyroid must also be monitored.

AIDS-Related Eye Diseases

Thanks to new discoveries and treatments, patients with acquired immune deficiency syndrome (AIDS) are living longer. But many of them are also going blind.

Recent developments in AIDS treatment have allowed patients to live longer, and doctors are seeing more effects of the deadly AIDS virus on the eyes. AIDS patients have a compromised immune system, and have difficulty defending themselves against even minor infections. As a result, certain eye infections that will not threaten the sight of healthy people can blind an AIDS patient.

The most common cause of blindness among AIDS sufferers is cytomegalovirus (CMV) retinitis, a progressive disease that destroys the retina. Foscarnet (trisodium phosphonoformate) is a relatively new drug developed in France that has been proven effective against CMV in a number of clinical tests. Another promising drug is Gancyclovir.

As doctors learn more about AIDS and how it can affect the

eyes, many of them are advising people who have been exposed to the virus to have their eyes checked every two or three months.

Dry Eyes

When your eyes are dry and itchy, it usually means that you're not producing enough of the right kind of tears, the kind that lubricate your eyes.

Normally there is a slow, steady production of tears that flow evenly over the eye from top to bottom. This lubricating "basal" tear secretion comes from tear glands located just above the eyes or in the upper conjunctiva. They are known as the lacrimal glands and accessory lacrimal glands. (There is also a "reflex" tear secretion, which enables you to produce tears when you see Bambi's mother die—or when there is sand or a fist in your eyes.)

Without basal tear lubrication, the whites of your eyes can become dry, bloodshot, and just plain sore. That's because your tears are more than just water. They are actually complex substances that form three different layers of protection across the eyes.

The outer layer is an oily liquid that spreads out over the entire surface of the eyes and helps prevent the watery layer of tears beneath it from evaporating too fast. The oily layer is produced by small glands at the edge of the eyelids called the meibomian glands. If these oil glands are plugged up, you may develop a chalazion (discussed earlier in this chapter).

The watery layer, which is what we normally think of when we say tears, is beneath the oily layer. Produced by the small glands in the upper conjunctiva as well as the large lacrimal glands—the major tear glands—this watery layer keeps the eyes moist and clean and washes away most irritants and foreign particles such as sand or pollen.

Closest to the eye itself is the mucin layer. This mucin, which is produced by cells in the conjunctiva known as goblet cells, spreads the tears evenly over the entire surface of the eye and helps hold the watery layer in place. Without it, the watery layer would break up quickly, leaving dry spots on the surface of the eye.

Most cases of dry eyes are caused by a lack of watery tears. There are many reasons for this lack. Medications such as antihistamines and diuretics can be responsible. Two other common causes are a lack of moisture in the air and old age. As the body gets older, tear production decreases. Vitamin A deficiency also can cause severe dry eyes; a lack of this nutrient is a leading cause of blindness in less-developed countries.

Sjögren's syndrome is characterized by dry eyes, dry mouth, and an autoimmune disease, especially rheumatoid arthritis. An inflammation of the tear-producing glands and the

Drugs That Can Cause Dry Eyes

The American Academy of Ophthalmology says the following drugs can cause dry eyes. If you already have dry eyes, these medications can make the condition even worse. The drugs are listed here by their generic names, but brand names may be different, so check with your doctor or pharmacist if you are concerned about a particular drug that has been prescribed for you.

If you are taking one of these drugs for only a short time, using artificial tears while you are on the drug should take care of your dry eye problem. If, however, you are taking one of them on a long-term basis, talk it over with your doctor.

- Acetophenazine
- Amitriptyline
- Antazoline
- Atropine
- Azatadine
- Belladonna
- Beta blockers
- Brompheniramine
- Carbinoxamine
- Carphenazine
- Chlorisondamine
- Chlorpheniramine
- Chlorpromazine
- Clemastine
- Cyroheptadine
- Dexbrompheniramine
- Dexchlorpheniramine
- Diethazine
- Dimethindene
- Doxylamine
- Ethopropazine
- Fluphenazine

salivary glands can reduce tear production as well as cause dryness in the mouth, nose, and throat. Rheumatoid arthritis or lupus also often accompany the condition. Sjögren's syndrome is considered an autoimmune disease, one in which the body's immune system attacks the moisture-producing glands as well as the joints.

While dry eyes can affect men or women at any age, the most likely victim is a woman either at or past middle age.

While you can probably figure out for yourself if you have dry eyes—the dry, scratchy sensation should be the first clue—you might not be able to tell what's causing it. An ophthalmologist can.

If the dry eyes are caused by a temporary condition—a visit

- Hexamethonium
- Homatropine
- Imipramine
- Isoretinoin
- Mesoridazine
- Methdilazine
- Methotrimeprazine
- Methscopolamine
- Methyldopa
- Methylthiouracil
- Metoprolol
- Morphine
- Nitrous oxide
- Nortriptyline
- Oxprenolol
- Perazine
- Periciazine
- Perphenazine
- Pheniramine
- Piperacetazine
- Practolol
- Prochlorperazine
- Promazine
- Promethazine
- Propiomazine
- Propranolol
- Protriptyline
- Pyrilamine
- Scopolamine
- Tetrahydrocannabinol (THC)
- Thiethylperazine
- Thiordazine
- Thirpropazate
- Trichloroethylene
- Trifluoperazine
- Trifupromazine
- Trimeprazine
- Tripelennamine
- Triprolidine

to the desert, a long flight in an airplane, a reaction to a drug—the condition should disappear when the reasons for it do. But most people with dry eyes have the problem all their lives.

The most common solution for the lack of the liquid is a solution of the liquid you lack—artificial tears. There are numerous brands of artificial tears available, and you don't need a prescription. Try several different ones and then stick with the one you like best. You may use them as often as necessary; once or twice a day, once or twice an hour—whatever helps.

Another way to help alleviate the condition is to keep your surroundings from being too dry. Use a humidifier to add moisture to your home. When you go outside on a dry day, wear wraparound sunglasses to prevent the moisture in your eyes from evaporating. And if you use a hair dryer, aim it at your hair, not your eyes.

You can also try various ointments, especially at night when the ointment film won't disturb your vision too much. One application of lubricating ointment before bed has more staying power than several drops of tears, and you won't have to get up during the night to put more in.

Your doctor may suggest sealing the tear drainage to prevent the tears that are produced from draining away too fast. Because the tears leave the eyes through the tiny openings at the inner lid margins and then flow down into the nose, closing off their escape route to help keep your eyes moister longer can be done on either a temporary or permanent basis.

Whatever the approach, the important thing is to reduce the dryness and irritation so that your eyes are once again moist and "see-worthy."

CHAPTER 7

INJURIES AND ACCIDENTS
FRISBEES, SQUASH BALLS, AND OTHER HAZARDS

I spy something with my little eye . . . something that is black and blue.

From a children's game

POW! SLAM! THWACK! THUD! and OOOF! when accompanied by lots of breaking furniture—of course—usually leaves the comic book hero with nothing worse than a black eye that can be quickly cured by putting a raw steak over it. The damage can't even be noticed in the next scene.

Pity it isn't that simple in real life.

Let's look at the reality of the situation.

Although the eyes are set back relatively deeply in the skull and are protected by the cheekbones, the nose, and the ridge of bone underneath the eyebrows—as well as the eyelids—they can and do come in fairly frequent contact with flying squash balls, Frisbees, and fists. Not to mention coat hangers, doors, a baby's fingers, champagne corks, firecrackers, broken glass, and a list of other objects long and varied enough to make reading a hospital emergency room's "cause of accident" survey interesting, informative, and at times tragically sad or embarrassingly funny.

The eyeball itself is a rather tough and resilient organ. If the injury is mild, the eye heals rapidly. If, however, the damage is severe, it can lead to blindness.

Let's consider some of the more common causes of eye injuries, how they are treated, and—more important—how they might be prevented.

Most types of eye injury have been around for as long as there have been eyes. After all, it doesn't make much difference to the eye whether it is hit with a state-of-the-art, computer-controlled plastic Frisbee or with a caveman's club. The reaction is still the same: Ouch! Other types of injury and potential injury are uniquely a product of our technology, though. Our ancestors didn't have to worry, for example, about welding torches or sunlamps.

Regardless of the type of injury or how modern its cause, there will be times when you aren't sure if you should immediately seek medical assistance or not. Each case is different, but as a general rule, when in doubt, *see your doctor*. And never adopt a "wait-and-see" attitude, because if you wait too long you just might never see again.

While we cannot tell you when you do not need to seek medical attention, we can tell you when you should. If any one of these conditions is present as the result of an injury, see your doctor.

- Pain and redness
- Pain plus a discharge from the eyes
- Blurred or double vision
- Any loss of vision
- A layer of blood between the cornea and the iris
- An eye that does not move as freely and completely as the other eye
- When one eye is protruding farther forward than the other
- When one pupil's size or shape is abnormal compared to the other eye

- A cut or penetration of either the eyelid or eyeball
- Spots, streaks, "flashing lights," or anything else that interferes with or obscures your vision, whether or not they are accompanied by pain.

Can VDTs Injure the Eyes?

There has been no proof that video display terminals (VDTs) emit enough of any sort of radiation to injure anyone's eyes. But VDT users do have legitimate complaints. The most frequent ones are eye fatigue, eye irritation, and blurred vision. Next come the complaints of tired, itching, burning, or watering eyes; headaches; flickering sensations; and double vision.

VDT users also complain about back, neck, or shoulder pain or stiffness. This is usually a result of poor posture or sitting at a desk that wasn't designed for computer work.

Poor design is also a problem in terms of lighting. Too much light can "wash out" a screen or cause glare. This can lead to eyestrain, as can working without enough light.

If you already wear glasses, you might want to have a "VDT tint" added to your lenses. This is a light tint that blocks out about 20 percent of the light. An antiglare coating can also help.

When it comes to actual eye problems, the main one is eye fatigue. The human eye was not built to focus on one small screen for hours at a time. That's why one of the best "cures" for VDT-related eye problems is a 15-minute break from looking at the screen every hour.

Sometimes, reading or magnifying glasses can be used to put your VDT screen in perfect focus. This way the glasses do the focusing instead of your eyes. This is especially helpful for people over 40.

Most reading glasses are designed to put things in sharp focus at the normal reading distance—16 inches. VDT screens are usually 21 inches from the eyes. Therefore, a slightly different reading prescription—usually a weaker one—will be needed for computer work.

The human eye is "at rest" when looking off into the distance. That's why staring out the window is so relaxing. It's not only the view that's good for you, but the fact that the eye doesn't have to work at focusing on anything up close.

A Black Eye

Despite what you see on TV or in the movies, and no matter how many funny stories or cartoons you've seen, a black eye is no joke, no matter what the cause of the injury—a flying fist, a swinging door, a pointing finger, or a popping champagne cork (see "Beware Those Popping Corks" on the opposite page).

The dark color and swelling that surround the injured orb are caused by damaged blood vessels and bleeding under the skin.

At times there can even be bleeding within the eye itself that leads to a hyphema, a buildup of blood behind the cornea. If that bleeding continues, the anterior chamber of the eye can fill with blood. Pressure may build up and damage the optic nerve. If the blood is not absorbed, it may have to be "washed out" by a surgical operation. In effect, a "simple" black eye can turn into a form of glaucoma that is extremely difficult to treat.

Every year countless men, women, and children suffer major eye damage—and blindness—due to "simple" black eyes.

If you do get a black eye, and if you also just happen to have the "traditional" raw steak handy, you'd be better off barbecuing the steak as a treat for yourself—after you've used an ice pack on your eye.

How did the idea of placing a raw steak over a black eye as a "cure" get started? No one really knows for sure, but it could be because raw meat, when properly stored in a refrigerator, is cold. It's the cold that can reduce the swelling, not the meat. Also, a steak is floppy, so it will conform to fit the face. But there are problems with this age-old remedy, problems such as the high cost of steak (especially when compared to the cost of ice cubes); bacteria on the steak, which could infect the eye; and the general yuckiness of covering your face with red, raw, and bleeding meat.

Stick with an ice pack.

The ice pack should be applied gently around the eye for about 15 minutes. Repeat this every hour as needed. But do not put pressure on the eye itself. The coldness will constrict the blood vessels of the eyelids and reduce bleeding and swelling.

You should also have a doctor look at your eye, especially if you experience any change in your normal vision such as blurriness or double images.

Beware Those Popping Corks

For those who consider champagne and other sparkling wines to be synonymous with festive occasions, the pop of the champagne cork is an important part of the ritual that makes imbibing the bubbly stuff so much fun.

If you're not careful how you open the bottle, however, you can get bleary-eyed—and bloody eyed—even before you drink the first drop.

That's because popping champagne corks are a lot like the BB guns your mother always warned you about when you were a kid. They can put your eye out.

There are seven things to remember about opening a bottle of champagne.

1. Keep the bottle chilled. A warm bottle is more likely to blow its cool—and its cork—than a properly chilled bottle.

2. Don't shake the bottle!

3. Before opening, peel the foil off the cork, and then hold the cork in place with your hand while you peel back the wire hood.

4. Place a towel over the bottle top and cork.

5. Twist the cork to break the seal. If the cork is stuck, run cool tap water over it for about 30 seconds or so and try again.

6. Make sure the cork is not aimed at anyone or at anything breakable.

7. Slowly twist and pull the cork out of the bottle.

Even though this method produces a more muted "pop" when the bottle is opened, it does retain more of the carbonation and will keep the bubbly bubblier longer.

Lacerations

Knife wounds, gunshot wounds, and explosions can do serious and permanent damage to both you and your eyes.

If the eyeball is perforated, aqueous humor leaks out. The front part of the eye can collapse in much the same way that a bean bag collapses when some of the beans leak out. And that's only part of the problem. The same rip, tear, or hole that lets the aqueous humor out can also let infection in. Bacteria entering the eye can cause endophthalmitis, a potentially blinding infection.

A perforated eye is a medical emergency. Do not attempt to wash or irrigate the eye. If the object that perforated the eye is still stuck there, leave it for a doctor to deal with. Pulling it out could cause the loss of more fluid and lead to more damage.

The eye should be covered at once with a loosely fitting patch or metal shield. Then the patient must be rushed to a doctor—or emergency room—immediately so that the laceration can be sewn up and the pressure within the eye restored.

The alternatives to immediate medical treatment are glaucoma, infection, and blindness.

Foreign Bodies in the Eye

Small particles can enter the eye on a windy day, or while you're driving with the window open, riding a bike, or jogging down the lane. A foreign body is usually quickly washed out of the eye by a flood of tears and the windshield-washer action of the eyelids. The wiper effect forces the particle off to the side of the eye and onto the eyelash or the eyelid.

It is the sharp-edged particle that can cause serious problems. Bits of metal, wood splinters, or chips of paint or stone can become lodged in the cornea or under the upper lid, producing a painful and persistent irritation. This type of injury is common among mechanics, construction workers, and tool-and-dye or lathe operators.

If something like this should happen to you, remember what your mother told you: "Don't rub it!" The first thing to do is blink. That might be enough to dislodge the speck.

If blinking doesn't work, lift the upper lid over the lower lid and blink a few more times. This lets the eyelashes of the lower lid brush the inside of the upper lid, possibly discharging any speck that is stuck there. If that doesn't work, keep the eye closed until you can get help.

It is often impossible for people to remove these particles themselves, no matter how long they spend irrigating or flushing out the eye. If a friend or a coworker can help, let them. If not, get to a doctor—fast.

Although these injuries are common and can be extremely painful, the treatment is relatively simple, and infections or other complications are few. Once the particle is removed, the eye usually heals in just a few days with the help of dilating drops and antibiotics.

Although treatment for this type of injury is simple, the very best policy is prevention. If your job or hobby puts your eyes in this type of danger, wear protective, industrial-strength eyeglasses or eye guards.

If you already wear glasses, you can get safety lenses ground to your prescription or nonprescription eye guards that will fit over your glasses. If you're out jogging or bicycling in sandy areas during the day, wear sunglasses. They can protect your eyes from more than just sunshine.

If you have only one good eye, you might want to wear some sort of eye protection all the time, no matter what you are doing, and choose your sports or other activities with extreme care.

Ultraviolet Burns

We've already discussed the dangers of UV light and the damage it can do to the cornea in the section on sunglasses (see chapter 3). But the sun is not the only UV source.

Sunlamps and tanning beds also produce UV light (see "How to Tan without Burning Your Eyes" on page 94). So do arc welding torches and some lasers. If you must use a sunlamp, a laser, a tanning bed, or a welding torch, make sure your eyes are protected.

A UV burn can cause an abnormal sensitivity to light, blurred vision or blindness, a sandy sensation in the eyes, and pain—lots of pain.

How to Tan without Burning Your Eyes

A tanning bed or sunlamp can give your entire body a pleasant glowing tan or a nasty and painful glowing burn—and your eyes are two of the first parts of the body that can be burned.

Unless you want to join the thousands of people who have learned just how painful and lasting "sunburned eyes" can be, there are three simple rules to follow.

1. Always wear the special goggles provided or recommended by the sunlamp's or tanning bed's manufacturer. If they are not available, use other goggles (not glasses, goggles!) which fit snugly around the eyes and block out potentially blinding UV radiation. Never use sunglasses or cotton balls as substitutes. They do not adequately protect the eyes.

2. Staying under a sunlamp or tanning bed longer than the manufacturer's recommendation will not give you a faster tan. It will give you a fast burn.

3. If you experience any of the eye burn symptoms—redness, light sensitivity, blurry vision, or pain—stop tanning immediately and see your eye doctor.

Follow these rules regardless of which type of tanning device you use. Sunlamps are usually labeled as producing either UVA or UVB radiation. Natural sunlight contains both types. Even though UVA sunlamps are the most popular because they screen out more of the UVB (often referred to as the "burning" radiation), both types can be dangerous if not used properly.

If you're having problems under the sunlamp or tanning bed even while following all the rules, your diet—or your medication or cosmetics—might be causing the trouble. Certain chemicals can make eyes more sensitive to UV radiation. Some of the more common photosensitizing chemicals are found in celery, citrus fruits, birth control pills, antibiotics, high blood pressure medication, antihistamines, and in some cosmetics. So if you are having problems, you might want to talk to your pharmacist or doctor.

Fortunately, a UV burn rarely leads to permanent blindness. With the aid of dilating eyedrops and a tight eye patch, the cornea usually heals in a few days. The eyedrops are used to relax the muscles of the iris and ciliary body. The tight eye patch is to prevent painful blinking, which can slow down the healing process.

Chemical Burns

We're all familiar with the dangers of hazardous industrial chemicals, and we usually assume that those dangerous chemicals are in factories far away from us and our children.

Wrong! Often the main differences between a hazardous industrial chemical and a helpful household cleaner is the size of the container or the name that's on the label.

You have to wonder, for example, why the word *chlorine* conjures up such horrifying images when it's talked about in terms of leaking out of a crashed railroad car, and yet it produces such pleasant and sweet-smelling images when talked about in terms of "New and Improved Super Duper Sudso Cleano with *Chlorine* Added!"

Chlorine is just one of the chemicals that can be found in many household cleaners and solvents. Many of these chemicals can burn the eye's delicate tissues after only a few seconds of exposure. Acids and alkalis are among the most dangerous. Acids usually cause extremely painful burns to the surface of the eye. Alkalis, such as ammonia, can penetrate the eye in a matter of seconds and destroy vision.

It is important that tight-fitting goggles be worn whenever you handle any dangerous chemicals. If a chemical does get in your eye, act fast. You have to irrigate the eye immediately.

One simple treatment is to simply stick your face—with your injured eye open—in a sink full of clean water and swish the water around. An even better treatment is to stick your eye under running water: a faucet, a drinking fountain, or an eye wash fountain. Use your fingers to keep the eye open, and roll your eyeball as much as possible to wash the chemical out.

The eye should be washed for at least 15 minutes for acid burns and at least 30 minutes for alkali burns. In the case of *any* chemical burn, the eye should also be examined by a doctor after the irrigation has been completed.

Sports
and Industrial Injuries

In the United States alone, approximately 500 children will hurt their eyes today. Another 500 hurt their eyes yesterday, and still another 500 will hurt theirs tomorrow, and the day after tomorrow, and so on. Some of them will wind up blind.

All told, more than 167,000 children will suffer eye injuries in the United States this year. Most of these will take place while the child is playing or involved in sports, because most sports are potentially dangerous. Baseball, basketball, tennis, squash, hockey—all can lead to eye injuries, sometimes blinding eye injuries.

Even children who manage to grow up without suffering any sort of eye injury are not home free. Every day adults who work for a living suffer about 1,000 industrial eye injuries. In fact, about 19 percent of all eye accidents happen on the job. Auto accidents are responsible for an additional 8 percent of all eye injuries.

When you combine childhood accidents, work-related injuries, sports injuries, injuries at home, and those from traffic accidents, more than one million Americans suffer some sort of eye injury every year. And nearly half of them happen at home.

Eye injuries are among the most common injuries treated in hospital emergency rooms. Yet 90 percent of all eye injuries could have been—and should have been—prevented.

The following preventive tips have been compiled from advice offered by the American Academy of Ophthalmology, the American Optometric Association, and the National Society to Prevent Blindness.

In the House

Before you do anything in your home, be sure you can see what you're doing. Make sure you have plenty of light in every room, hallway, and stairwell in the house—including the basement, garage, attic, and any other space people use. Some other tips include:

Protective Eye Wear: It's Part of the Game

In the mid-1970s, there were more than 70,000 ice hockey–related eye injuries reported every year. Today, thanks to the helmets that are now required in the different leagues—those for the kiddies all the way up to the pros—the number is almost negligible.

Helmets, face guards, goggles, and safety glasses do work to prevent or at least limit the results of accidents at home, at work, or at play.

Most safety lenses for both industry and sports wear are made of polycarbonate, the toughest lens material available today. Once used to make bulletproof windows, polycarbonate weighs about half as much as glass, and when coated with scratch-resistant materials, it is even more resistant to welding splatter and pitting than glass is.

The sort of eye protection you need will determine how thick the lenses should be. If you don't need corrective glasses, or if you wear contact lenses, you can get your protective lenses "plain." If you have a vision problem, you can have them ground to your prescription.

To make sure you are getting safety eye wear meeting the stringent American National Standards Institute Z87 standards, look for a Z87 etched on the lenses.

Glass safety lenses are also available. They offer better protection from infrared radiation and are less likely to be damaged by chemical splatter than plastic or polycarbonate lenses.

But whether you're looking at glasses or goggles, the lenses are only part of the protection process. The frames are also important. You might consider sports frames featuring padded or rubber bridges and deep-grooved eye wires to make sure the lenses don't fall out if they get hit. You can also get frames that have been formed to give you a wider field of vision and with an attached headband so they don't fly off your face.

● Make sure all spray nozzles—whether they be on cans of hair spray, deodorant, or oven cleaner—are aimed where you want the spray to go before you press the button. Be especially careful when using hair spray to keep it away from your eyes.

- Carefully read all instructions before using any cleaning fluids, detergents, ammonia, or other harsh chemicals. Once you're done using them, wash your hands.
- Use grease shields on frying pans to reduce splattering.
- If you have a sunlamp in the house, make sure you also have goggles to protect your eyes—and use them.

In the Workshop

Workshop clutter is a contributing factor in many workshop accidents. Even when you do have enough light to see by, it won't do you much good if everything is buried under a layer of scrap wood, paper, parts, and tools. And here are some other precautions:

- Wear safety goggles or glasses.
- Read, understand, and follow the instructions for any tools or chemicals you use.
- Think about protecting your eyes—and the rest of your body—from flying fragments, sawdust, fumes, dust particles, sparks, and splashes before you begin work.

At Play

Based on past records, more than 6,000 toy-related eye injuries will be carefully wrapped and waiting under the Christmas tree this year in the form of slingshots, skateboards, and other unsafe toys.

According to experts, more than 1,000 of those injuries will be caused by BB guns. It is worth remembering—and repeating as often as required—that BB guns are not toys. They are weapons.

Toys and BB guns are not the only causes of childhood eye injuries. Screwdrivers, nails, rocks, sticks, and stones also blind children every year, especially when thrown or fallen on. Just as some toys are more dangerous than others, some children are more at risk than others. Boys are more likely to suffer eye injuries than girls, especially older boys who don't wear glasses.

(Even though normal eyeglasses are not as strong or sturdy as protective or safety lenses, they do offer some protection.) Here are more safety considerations:

- Do not let young children play with toys or games that could blind them or the children they are playing with. Young children do not need darts, fireworks, BB or pellet guns, or toys with sharp edges.
- If children are playing with toys or games that could be dangerous, make sure that you or another responsible adult is there to supervise them.
- Teach children the safe way to use potentially dangerous items such as scissors, knives, sticks, and pencils.

On the Job

According to the U.S. Department of Labor, three out of every five people who suffer an on-the-job eye injury were not wearing any safety eye wear at all, and three-quarters of these victims later admitted that they did not feel it was necessary—at least not until the accident. Those injured while wearing some sort of safety eye wear were wearing items offering inadequate protection.

In many cases and for many types of jobs, there is little difference between the types of safety eye wear needed and the types worn in the home workshop or garden or for sports. There is, however, a wider variety of safety eye wear made to meet the broader range of safety needs in industry. These include:

- Eye shields that attach to safety glasses to protect the wearer from dust, flying particles, or sparks that could enter the eye from the top, bottom, or sides of the lenses. In effect, these shields convert safety glasses to safety goggles.
- Goggles that allow only indirect airflow to protect the eyes from chemicals, molten metals, and other materials that could splash as well as from dust, sparks, and flying particles.
- Face shields that provide splash protection for the entire face. They should be worn on top of goggles because they are not built to withstand a heavy impact.

- Welding or laser goggles or shields that are specifically designed to protect the eyes from the intense heat, rays, sparks, and flying debris produced by electrical arcs, welding torches, or lasers.

An Eye Safety Program for the Workplace

Because most large corporations can afford to keep a full-time safety director, they often have a much lower accident rate than smaller companies. But regardless of the size of the company, no employer can afford to do without a safety program, a program that also deals with eye safety. That is why more and more companies are retaining an optometrist or ophthalmologist as a consultant.

According to the American Optometric Association, an effective industrial eye safety program should:

- Identify eye-hazardous jobs and areas and make employees aware of them.
- Identify all workers holding eye-hazardous jobs or required to be in eye-hazardous areas, even if only to walk through them.
- Determine and specify the appropriate protective eye wear for each task and/or area.
- Provide appropriate on-the-job protective eye wear, including prescription safety eye wear if needed, to employees at no cost.
- Provide an ongoing program to educate and remind employees about the importance of wearing eye-protective equipment.
- Provide procedures for the regular inspection of eye-protective equipment and the replacement of any that is damaged.
- Be based on an established common policy regarding the use of eye safety equipment. Some companies make the wearing of eye safety equipment a mandatory condition of employment.
- Identify the enforcement staff and specify their responsibilities and authority.
- Be published in one document that is distributed and explained fully to employees.

In the Garden

More than 5,000 people suffer eye injuries every year while working in their gardens. Here's how to avoid some of the hazards:

- Do not let anyone stand on the side of or in front of a moving lawnmower.
- Pick up rocks and stones before mowing your lawn. These stones could be picked up by a lawnmower's blades and thrown out of the front, sides, or back of the mower, causing a serious injury.
- If you use any sort of pesticides, make sure the nozzles are pointed away from your face, and when you are done using these chemicals, wash your hands.
- Wear safety goggles or glasses when pruning bushes or trees, chopping wood, or using a chain saw.
- Avoid low-hanging branches.

Around the Car

Automobiles can explode. If you need light to look in your gas tank, for example, or at your battery, use a flashlight.

If you have to jump start your car, be especially careful. Remember to:

- Keep a pair of safety goggles with your jumper cables, and wear them. Battery acid can cause serious eye injuries.
- Make sure that the two cars are not touching one another.
- Be sure that the jumper cable clamps never touch one another.
- Never lean over the battery when attaching the cables.
- Attach one end of the positive (red) cable to the positive terminal of the dead battery first, and then attach the other end to the good battery.
- Attach the negative (black) cable to the negative terminal of the good battery and then and only then attach the other end to a grounded area on the engine away

from the negative terminal of the dead battery. Never attach a cable to the negative terminal of the dead battery.

Around Fireworks

Fireworks maim, blind, and kill people—thousands of people every year. Every year the number of victims increases. According to the Consumer Product Safety Commission, two-thirds of all fireworks victims are under age 21. More than one-fourth are under age 10. Heed these warnings:

- Never use explosive fireworks.
- Never allow children to ignite any fireworks.
- Do not stand near anyone who is igniting any fireworks.

In Sports

When it comes to sports-related eye injuries, the dangers vary with age. Statistics show that the most frequent source of such injuries for children between the ages of 5 and 14 is baseball. Basketball is the leading cause for those between the ages of 15 and 24. Once you pass 25, the racquet sports are most likely to be the culprits.

Baseball. One in five sports-related eye injuries takes place on a baseball diamond, thanks in part to the simple fact that most pitchers—kids and professionals—can pitch better than most batters can duck.

If baseball is your game, a batting helmet and sports goggles should be part of it.

Basketball. The most dangerous place to be in a basketball game is beneath the backboard while a zillion elbows, arms, hands, and fingers are all scrambling for the rebound.

After suffering two serious eye injuries beneath the backboards, L.A. Lakers–great Kareem Abdul Jabbar started wearing protective goggles. You don't have to be a great athlete to wear goggles, just a smart one.

Racquet sports. A racquetball in play can reach speeds in excess of 120 miles per hour. And while the racquet itself (whether it be for racquetball, squash, tennis, or even badminton) rarely goes quite that fast, if it hits you in the eye it can blind you as quickly and as permanently as any ball can.

In fact, while the greatest threat in tennis is the tennis ball, in squash and racquet ball it's the racquet itself—and the bodies of the other players.

Your best bet is shatter-resistant sports goggles. The U.S. Squash Racquet Association requires that eye guards be worn at all professional and amateur squash tournaments, a rule that more and more racquet clubs are following for even league or casual games.

And don't forget. If you need glasses to see clearly in general, you'll need them even more on the courts. The balls and racquets fly fast—and hard—enough to do serious damage to any part of the body that they hit.

Contact sports. If you box, fence, practice karate, or play football, soccer, ice or field hockey, lacrosse, or any other contact sport, there is protective eye wear available. You can use it, or you can risk having your eyes battered by balls, pucks, sticks, knees, elbows, fingers, ice skates, feet, and cleats.

Golf. A golf ball in the head can ruin your day—and your sight. The best defense is being aware of what's going on around you. And don't stand too close to the person making a shot; a golf club in the face isn't too much fun either.

Skiing, hiking, and climbing. The more you ski, the greater your chances of developing snow blindness, thanks to all the UV light. The UV light has two chances to get you. First it hits you as it comes down from the sun. Then it has another chance at you as it reflects off the snow.

Wearing snow goggles isn't always enough. You should wear the right type of goggles for the region you are skiing in. Experts say that lenses with light tints are better for the flat light on the slopes of ski resorts in the eastern United States, while darker tints should be worn in the western part of the country because the sunlight is much more intense there.

Hikers and mountain climbers can have similar problems. And the higher your altitude—whether skiing or hiking—the more likely your eyes are to suffer a UV burn.

If you're above 10,000 feet, you could also wind up suffering from high-altitude illness, which can cause retinal hemorrhages and blurry vision. If you go above 15,000 feet, you also risk high-altitude retinopathy, which can develop when a lack of oxygen and reduced atmospheric pressure causes blood vessels in the retina to leak or rupture. It can result in temporary partial blindness.

Climbing to that height slowly, thus giving your body a chance to adjust to the changes, reduces the odds of getting hit with the problem. Exercising vigorously at high altitudes increases the risk.

In any event, the condition usually clears up on its own once the climber has come down and spent a few days with both feet firmly planted somewhere around sea level.

Fishing. Like skiers who spend their days on highly reflective snow, fishing aficionados who spend their days on highly reflective lakes or streams risk serious UV eye burns from both direct sunlight and reflected sunlight.

And that's just what the light can do to you.

A flying fish hook can cut right through your eyeball. A poke in the eye from the tip of a fishing pole can also make you wish you'd fished at a place that serves them with chips and ketchup.

Swimming. Goggles should be as much a part of your swimming gear as your bathing suit is. Chlorine and other chemicals in pools can irritate the eyes, but the irritation is temporary. Bacteria, viruses, and amoebas commonly found in swimming holes can also cause a problem.

While your goggles have to fit snugly to keep the water out of your eyes, make sure that they aren't too tight. If they are, you could wind up with a "goggles migraine." It's a throbbing headache that shows up an hour or two after swimming, apparently caused by pressure on the nerves around the eyes.

Hunting. As a rule, eye guards aren't going to stop a stray bullet, an arrow, or a charging bear. So when it comes to vision care and hunting, the emphasis is on good vision—for you and everyone else running around out there with a loaded weapon. You don't want to be mistaken for a trophy, not even one worthy of the taxidermist.

Keep in mind that many color-blind people can't see any difference between red and green, especially in poor light or at dusk. The safest and most visible color to wear is orange—the brighter the better.

Working out. Unless you have a tendency to run into barbells, working out is relatively safe as far as your eyes are concerned. But there are a couple of exceptions.

Straining can cause problems for people recovering from some eye operations. Ask your doctor what's best in your case.

Doing headstands or hanging upside down with gravity inversion boots may do wonders for your back, but those activities can also increase the blood pressure inside your retinal blood vessels as well as the pressure of the fluid within the eyeballs. As a rule, the pressure levels return to normal shortly after you turn yourself right side up again. If you are already prone to glaucoma or other eye or retinal problems, check with your eye doctor first.

On the other hand, studies have shown that normal exercising—jogging, cycling, and other activities done with your feet on the floor—may actually reduce intraocular pressure.

█ CHAPTER 8

CATARACTS
THESE VEILS
OF AGE CAN BE LIFTED

Mine eyes are dim,
I cannot see.
I have not brought
My specs with me.

—Old drinking song

The only way to guarantee that you'll never get cataracts is to die young. They are as much a part of life as gray hair, wrinkles, and liver spots. But cataracts, unlike other signs of advancing age, can be permanently removed, and the vision they once clouded can be restored.

A cataract occurs when the lens of the eye grows thicker, becoming cloudy and opaque. The aging process gradually turns the normally clear and transparent crystalline lens white or yellowish brown. Because this murkiness reduces the amount of light that can enter the eye, it also reduces your vision.

If you could watch the whole process through a microscope, you'd see that the lens of your eye is made up of cells and transparent fibers, which continue to grow throughout your entire life. With time, however, the fibers become compact and lose their transparency. As with other parts of your body, the eyes also can retain fluid, causing the lens to thicken or swell. All of these changes contribute to a loss of visual clarity.

These changes take time. It normally takes years to develop a cataract. And just as the timing may vary from person to person, so can the severity.

Cataracts can be so small that they have virtually no effect whatsoever on your vision. Many people live out their lives without doing anything about them. Conversely, however, they can leave you virtually blind.

While the aging process is responsible for most cataracts, there are other causes. These include injury, inflammation, and medication, especially cortisone.

Some babies are born with cataracts because of an inherited disease or problems during pregnancy. Mothers who contract rubella during the first trimester of pregnancy, for example, may give birth to babies with cataracts, hearing defects, and abnormalities of the heart. But thanks to the development of the rubella vaccine, "rubella babies" are no longer very common.

Studies also show that there may be a direct link between cataracts and excessive exposure to sunlight. Studies show that there appears to be a higher incidence of cataracts in geographic areas where sunlight—especially the UV light portion—is intense.

Does this mean that taking a holiday in the sun will doom you to looking at the world through cloudy eyes? No. What it does mean is that wearing sunglasses made to block out potentially harmful UV light rays is a wise precaution.

But once you have cataracts, it really doesn't make any difference what caused them. Just as an arm broken while rescuing a fair young damsel from distress will hurt as long and as much (and also take as long to heal) as one broken after a slip on an icy patch of pavement, the cause of a cataract has little if anything to do with the cure.

Options in a Blurry World

As cataracts develop, several things usually occur. The most common complaint is blurred vision. Activities that require sharp vision, such as reading and driving, become more difficult. Driving at night may become hazardous due to the glare of approaching headlights.

Other common complaints include sensitivity to light, actually feeling as if there is a film over your eyes, noticing a change in color of the pupil of your eyes, and needing frequent changes in glasses. Some people simply report that the world "looks dull."

When Clearer Vision Signals Trouble

It's one thing for senior citizens to feel that they're getting their youthful strength back. But if they feel they're getting their vision back, they could be in for trouble.

Older people sometimes think that this is happening to them because they find that they can do close work—such as reading the paper or even a phone book—without their reading glasses. What's really happening is that they are getting more nearsighted. And that can be an early sign of cataract development.

Of course, any or all of the above can also be signals that other eye problems are developing—problems such as macular degeneration (a deterioration of the retina that's discussed in chapter 12). The important thing to remember is that these symptoms indicate that you need to check with your eye doctor.

Let's say that you've gone to your doctor and the verdict *is* cataracts. What do you do next?

Well, maybe the answer is . . . nothing.

Living with cataracts can be compared to living with teenagers. Their potential to drive you absolutely, positively bonkers is ever present. The problem is always there, like a volcano quietly burping in the background. But some people live their entire lives without ever having their neighboring volcano or their in-house teenagers explode. Similarly, even though cataracts can lead to loss of vision, it is nearly always the kind of visual loss that can be reversed. And in other cases, cataracts develop so slowly that they never cause a major reduction in vision. An operation is unnecessary.

But just what is a major reduction in vision? That depends on you. Some people are quite willing to put up with a little blurred vision. Their occupation, attitude, and lifestyle let them live comfortably with their cataracts and the limits they place on their lives.

On the other hand, even a minor reduction in vision can be a major catastrophe for some people. Accountants, airline pilots, athletes, artists, machinists, and surgeons might find life and livelihood threatened by even a slight reduction in vision. They might need an operation at the first sign of a cataract.

So the decision to have surgery is a very personal one, based on how well you are functioning and how satisfied you are with the way things are. It is only rarely that a lens becomes so swollen that it absolutely, positively has to be removed. Often a change in glasses, or the regular use of eyedrops to dilate the pupils to let more light into the eyes, can forestall surgery for months—even years.

But if you decide that cataracts are imposing too many limits on the way you live and work, the only real solution is surgery. It would be nice if there were some sort of pill or potion we could take that would dissolve cataracts and make surgery unnecessary. There is currently a great deal of research in that very area. And there are numerous products on the market today that are supposed to delay cataract formation or even reverse it. The key words here are *supposed to*. These claims have been made about specific vitamins, amino acids, hormones, and even aspirin.

A Role for Vitamins C and E?

Even though there is no guarantee that anything will prevent cataracts from forming, or even delay them, there are indications that some vitamins may be able to help some people.

One research study showed that people who took 300 to 600 milligrams of vitamin C or 400 international units of Vitamin E daily for five years before turning 60 were less likely to develop cataracts after age 60. This is just one study, however, and more research needs to be done before any definite conclusions can be drawn.

Special "secret" or "wonder drug" injections, pills, and eyedrops have also been tried. So far, however, there is no compelling evidence to show that any of them can actually prevent cataracts from forming or reverse them once they have formed. At best, these chemicals and compounds might be harmless. At worst, they could damage what vision is left, or cause other serious medical problems.

This is not to say, however, that there will never be an anti-cataract pill or potion. There is a lot of research being done, and there have been some encouraging results. When rats are made diabetic, for example, they often develop cataracts. Drugs that inhibit an enzyme known as aldose reductase seem to prevent such cataracts from forming. This may or may not lead to successful drug treatment for human cataracts, but even if it does, the availability of such a drug is years away.

Surgery, however, does work, and it is available now. The surgeon will, as a rule, do only one eye at a time. Although cataracts usually develop in both eyes, one eye is usually worse than the other. The surgeon will often do that one first. After the first eye heals, you may be left with unbalanced vision until the second cataract is removed. When the second one heals, you can expect to once again have good binocular vision.

Restoring the Focus

In the operation, the surgeon removes the clouded lens. The good news is that a barrier to crisp, clear vision is gone. The bad news is that a powerful lens has been removed with it. Without the lens, light rays that enter your eye will not focus on the retina, but somewhere behind it, just as they do in a far-sighted eye (for a refresher on farsightedness, see chapter 3).

This leaves three corrective choices: special eyeglasses called cataract glasses, special contact lenses, or a new lens that can be surgically implanted in the eye. This new lens is called an intra-ocular lens (IOL) for the simple reason that *intraocular* means "inside the eye."

We'll go into all three alternatives in more detail shortly. But first, keep this is mind: Whatever method you choose depends on a number of circumstances, including your age, the presence of other eye diseases, the vision of your other eye, your ability to wear and manipulate a contact lens, and last but far from least, the skill of the surgeon performing the operation.

Now let's look at the three alternatives in more detail.

Glasses

Wearing special cataract glasses is the safest, simplest, least expensive, and oldest postsurgical solution. The main disadvantage is that there can be problems adjusting to them.

They are usually heavier and thicker than conventional eyeglasses. In fact, they look a lot like the bottom of a soda pop bottle. And they can produce visual distortion.

What you see through cataract glasses is usually enlarged. Straight lines appear somewhat curved, and peripheral vision is blocked out. As a result, objects off to one side may suddenly loom into view. Not only do they appear "out of nowhere," (the "jack-in-the-box" effect), they loom about 25 percent larger than life when they do.

Contact Lenses

Contact lenses are also quite safe, but they too can be difficult to adjust to. It's hard enough for a young person to learn how to use and manipulate contact lenses. For older people— and they are the ones who need them—the task can be almost insurmountable when combined with arthritis or other ailments.

But many older people decide it's worth the aggravation and effort, because contact lenses are such an improvement over cataract glasses. There is practically no enlargement of the image or loss of peripheral vision.

Since handling contact lenses can be the major problem for elderly people, extended-wear lenses—which need to be removed, cleaned, and replaced only about once a week—avoid many of the difficulties and much of the bother of daily-wear lenses.

As with any other contact lenses, however, you should be

alert for and aware of unusual redness of the eye, excessive watering, light sensitivity, or any eye pain. If problems do occur, check with your doctor immediately.

Intraocular Lenses (Implanted Lenses)

Intraocular lenses, or IOLs, represent one of the most beneficial developments in the field of eye surgery. These plastic lenses are about the size and shape of normal, plastic, hard contact lenses, but they have tiny flexible feet, or "haptics," attached to the edges to hold them in place *inside* the eye. They are permanently inserted in the eye when the cataract is removed. They require no cleaning, replacement, or other maintenance and offer the patient virtually natural vision.

Intraocular lenses are manufactured with high precision and are ordered based on measurements of the length and curvature of the eye. Because any corrective power can be ordered, the ophthalmologist may select lenses that will correct the eye either for distance vision or near vision. Bifocal IOLs are not yet available (except in certain research studies), and their advantage over regular IOLs has not been established.

Sometimes the lens implant is not a perfect match, and a patient will still need corrective lenses—glasses or contact lenses—after the surgery. While it might seem odd at first, a patient can wear contact lenses over an implanted lens. That's because the implanted lens is underneath the surface of the eye and does not touch the contact lens.

Intraocular lenses were first developed in Europe and have been popular in North America since the mid–1970s. The results are generally quite good, and as surgeons become more experienced and lens-making technology improves, they will be even better.

Not everyone with a cataract is a candidate for an implant. People with certain preexisting eye problems, such as uveitis, might have to learn to live with conventional contact lenses or cataract glasses. Also, small children, whose eyes are still growing, are not good candidates. The size and power of their eyes may change as they get older.

Types of Cataract Surgery

Now that we have an overview of what can be done, let's take a more detailed look at the surgery itself. There are two main techniques for cataract surgery: intracapsular and extracapsular. In addition, some doctors now prefer a third procedure, phacoemulsification.

Intracapsular

With intracapsular surgery, the entire cataract and its surrounding capsule are removed. An incision is made in the upper part of the eye where the white and colored parts meet. The cornea is gently folded back. A freezing probe, a *cryoextractor*, is placed on the cataractous lens. The stiff, frozen lens is gently and carefully removed from the eye, and the incision is closed carefully with very fine stitches.

Extracapsular

The extracapsular method is similar to the intracapsular procedure except that the back part of the lens capsule, the clear membrane between the lens and interior of the eye, is left in place. An incision is made just as it would be for the intracapsular technique. The anterior, or front, surface of the lens is cut with a fine needle. Then the hard center of the lens (the nucleus) is carefully squeezed out with a gentle pressure and any remaining fragments of the cataractous lens (the cortex) are sucked out of the eye with a small suction device.

The posterior, or rear, of the capsule is left intact to prevent the vitreous, which is located behind the lens, from moving forward. The posterior capsule also provides some support for a lens implant. Within months of the original surgery, however, the posterior capsule might begin to cloud up, reducing vision once again.

In that case, the capsule can be opened with a knife or, even simpler, a laser beam. The type of laser used for this procedure is the neodymium-YAG laser (YAG stands for yttrium-aluminum-garnet), named for the material that produces the energy source of laser light. The laser procedure, which is not painful, is done in the doctor's office and takes only a few minutes.

Phacoemulsification

Phacoemulsification is a relatively new technique developed in the early 1970s. A special kind of probe—a *phacoemulsifier*—is used. The business end of the probe features a hollow titanium needle that vibrates about 40,000 times per second, breaking the cataract up and virtually liquefying it with ultrasonic vibrations.

The phacoemulsifier also functions as a vacuum cleaner, sucking the liquefied cataract from the eye.

The incision needed for the process is slightly smaller than the one used in a conventional extracapsular operation, so advocates of this procedure believe the healing process is a little faster.

Although it is a bit more difficult for the surgeon to learn, the technique is probably no better or worse than the other techniques. But those surgeons who are comfortable with it seem to prefer it.

Implanting the New Lenses

Once the cataract is removed, there is room for an intraocular lens to be permanently inserted. While there are hundreds of different types of IOLs that can be implanted, most of them fall within two broad categories: anterior chamber implants and posterior chamber implants.

Anterior chamber implants are placed just in front of the iris, while posterior implants are placed just behind it.

Although both techniques seem to work quite well, in recent years surgeons have seen more complications with anterior chamber lenses. This may be because they can rest on the iris and their haptics, or feet, come into direct contact with the drainage system for the fluid that percolates throughout the interior of the eye.

Posterior chamber implants are slightly more difficult to insert, but there are fewer complications, possibly because they do not come in direct contact with any of the critical structures inside the eye.

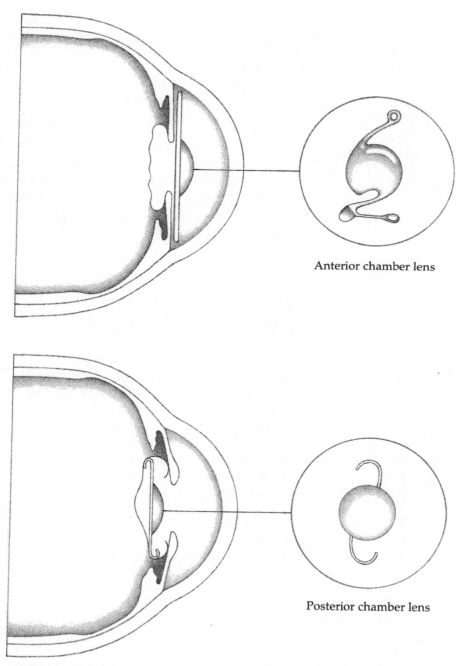

Anterior chamber lens

Posterior chamber lens

Following cataract removal, there are basically two lens implant options. An anterior chamber lens (top) rests in front of the iris. A posterior chamber lens (bottom) rests behind the iris.

Anterior chamber implants can be used whether your surgeon is using the intracapsular or extracapsular surgical technique. Posterior chamber implants can be used only if your surgeon uses the extracapsular procedure.

Most cataract surgeries performed today utilize the extracapsular approach coupled with posterior chamber implants. As a rule, there are few complications and the patient comes out of it with good vision.

Foldable lenses are a relatively new implant variation. Their advantage is that they can be folded, much like a taco shell, and inserted through a smaller incision. Such incisions would be expected to heal quickly and not cause much astigmatism. The "taco style" lenses seem to have good potential, but they are still being perfected.

If You're Facing Surgery, Here's What to Expect

Every operation, every surgeon, every patient, and every situation is different. But these general guidelines usually apply.

Most cataract surgeries are treated as outpatient procedures and done under local anesthesia, using the same type of numbing medication used by dentists. This anesthetic is injected in back of the ear or around the temple and then underneath the eye. Some patients and some doctors prefer a general anesthetic. Sometimes the decision is left to the patient.

The anesthetic performs three functions.

- It numbs the eye so you don't feel any pain.
- It prevents eye movement.
- It "shuts off" the vision in the eye so you can't see the surgeon or the scalpel he uses.

Depending on your surgeon and your situation, you might be asked to use antibiotic eyedrops or ointment for a few days prior to the surgery.

Special drops to dilate the pupil will usually be put in when you are being readied for the surgery. Dilating—expanding—the pupil makes it easier for the surgeon to see the cataract. You may also be given a mild tranquilizer to calm the nerves. You may be asked to take nothing by mouth for several hours before the operation. This is a standard precaution used before most types of surgery. If you do use regular medication or drink alcohol excessively, you should discuss this with your doctor in advance.

The skin around your eyes will be scrubbed with soap and alcohol, and a sterile cloth or paper drape will be put over your head and body. A tube is used to blow fresh air under the drape to make breathing easier.

All of these preparations can take as long as an hour. The operation itself—including the lens implant—usually takes less than an hour.

If you aren't spending the night in the hospital, and most people don't, make sure you have someone to drive you home. You will be wearing an eye patch covered with a metal shield to protect the eye from accidental injury. You might also have some discomfort, so the eye doctor may prescribe some pain pills or ask you to take over-the-counter pain medication for the first few days after the operation. Make sure you discuss in advance any other medication you might be taking. Keep in mind that drinking alcohol while taking pain pills could be dangerous.

The doctor will probably want to see you within a day or two of the operation and probably every one or two weeks for the next six weeks after that. Eyedrops will be used during this period to provide comfort, to speed the healing process, and to prevent infection. Glasses or a shield should be worn during the day to protect the eye from injury, and you should sleep with the shield on for the same reason.

Get plenty of rest and don't do any heavy lifting, straining, or other exercising until the doctor gives you permission. Too much strain could pop a blood vessel in your eye. It's usually okay to take a shower and wash your hair, but try to keep soap and water out of the convalescing eye.

You should be able to resume normal activities after about six weeks. At that time you should have your eyes checked for a new prescription for glasses or contact lenses.

Possible Complications

No surgical procedure comes with a 100 percent guarantee. Even though cataract surgery is usually a highly successful and trouble-free procedure, complications can and do occur. You should be aware of them.

Any time an incision is made in the eye, small blood vessels are cut. If the bleeding cannot be controlled, the eye may fill with blood and permanent damage may result.

Infection is also a rare possiblity. If bacteria enter the eye through an incision, endophthalmitis, the blinding infection discussed in chapter 6, can develop.

Sometimes, even though the operation is a success, the patient doesn't see as well as expected. When this happens, it is often because of fluid that collects in the center of the retina, the part responsible for central vision. This condition—known as cystoid macular edema—will sometimes clear up by itself, or after cortisone has been injected around the eye. Sometimes, however, it can't be cured, and the patient is left with good peripheral vision but poor central vision.

Retinal detachment, a rare but potentially blinding complication, can occur months or even years after cataract surgery. Retinal detachments seem to be less common when an extracapsular procedure is done, but the condition occurs so rarely for all types of cataract surgery that it is difficult to be sure.

All of these complications are scary. And while they are not likely, they are possible. If you keep them in mind and weigh them against the potential—and much more likely—benefits, you will be better able to make an intelligent decision about whether or not to undergo cataract surgery.

CHAPTER 9

GLAUCOMA
THE SNEAK THIEF
OF SIGHT

How soon hath Time, the subtle thief of youth
Stoln on its wing my three and twentieth
year.

John Milton

In the same way that high blood pressure can catch you unaware and rob you of your life, high eye pressure can sneak up on you and steal your sight. And like death, the blindness is permanent.

We are talking about glaucoma.

Glaucoma is the term applied to an entire family of diseases involving increased pressure within the eye. Not only is it an entire family of diseases, it is a disease that often runs in families. If anyone in your family has glaucoma or has gone blind or suffered any loss of vision for any mysterious reason—you should let your eye doctor know about it.

You should also ask the doctor how often you need regular checkups. The earlier glaucoma is diagnosed, the greater the chance of lowering your intraocular pressure and keeping your vision.

As you may remember from chapter 1, a watery fluid, the aqueous humor, is produced in the eye's posterior chamber by the ciliary body. This fluid percolates through the pupil into the anterior chamber, and then drains away at the anterior chamber angle, the point where the cornea, iris, and sclera all intersect. From there the fluid flows through a network of tiny channels, the trabecular meshwork, and into a larger collecting channel known as Schlemm's canal (named after an early pioneer in the anatomy of the eye).

From there the fluid enters the bloodstream. This process maintains an eye pressure of 15 to 20 millimeters of mercury inside the eye.

If you don't like the medical school explanation, try this one. Imagine a faucet that is turned on all the time. The water flows into a hose. As long as the other end of the hose is unplugged, there is no problem. But if you plug the other end, the water pressure will build up inside of the hose, and eventually the hose will be damaged.

As with the hose, if there is any sort of blockage that prevents the fluid from properly draining out of the eye, pressure builds up within the eye. In fact, the word *glaucoma* means "hard eyeball." The increased pressure in the eye leads to the gradual compression—and destruction—of the nerve fibers in the optic nerve.

One of the most frustrating and frightening aspects of glaucoma is that there are no early warning signs. The minor increases in eye pressure are usually not noticeable.

The most common indication that a person has glaucoma is partial blindness—irreversible blindness. Peripheral vision is usually the first to go. Then the field of remaining vision shrinks. If the pressure continues to build without being treated, a small island of vision is all that is left, and eventually this too is lost—forever.

There are more than 50,000 people in the United States alone who have been blinded by glaucoma—approximately 11 percent of all the blindness in the nation. There are also more than two million others who are being treated for the condition. Glaucoma strikes 1.5 percent of people over age 40, and between

15 and 20 percent of people over 70, but it hits blacks three times more frequently than it does whites. Blacks also get it at a younger age and suffer more severely from it.

Don't Confuse Migraine Effects with Glaucoma

Migraine headaches, like glaucoma, can steal your peripheral vision, at least temporarily.

According to some studies, nearly one-third of all migraine headache sufferers will lose some of their peripheral vision. While the elderly and long-term sufferers are the most likely to be affected, it can happen to anyone.

Even though doctors know that this loss of sight around the edges of the visual field does happen, they aren't 100 percent sure why. But it appears to stem from the fact that migraine headaches reduce the amount of blood that flows into the brain. This affects the optic nerve and the areas of the brain that deal with sight.

Checking Your Pressure

The effects of glaucoma cannot be reversed. As a result, most doctors concentrate on spotting it as early as possible and treating it to prevent further vision loss.

The blinding powers of glaucoma can be held in check through medication and—in some cases—surgery. But nothing can be done about it until it has been detected.

Just as we use a blood pressure cuff to check blood pressure, we use an eye pressure gauge—called a tonometer—to check eye pressure. The procedure, while unnerving at first, is simple and painless as long as it is done by qualified medical personnel. (Like home blood pressure testers, there are portable tonometers available for in-home use. Designed for properly trained patients, the briefcase-size instruments allow them to track fluctuations in eye pressure and monitor their own condition.)

First a drop of anesthetic is put on the eye itself, then the tonometer is used to measure the intraocular pressure—the pressure of the fluids inside the eye.

Older tonometers consist of a small gauge that actually touches the surface of the eye. Modern tonometers may also lightly touch the eye. But some merely shoot a puff of air into the eye to measure the pressure. The air-puff tonometers are simple to use and do not require anesthetic eyedrops.

If the pressure is 22 millimeters of mercury or greater, glaucoma should be suspected. If it's in the 30s or 40s, there is little doubt about it. Pressures can go as high as 70 or 80, but at these levels both the patient and the doctor usually know that there is something seriously wrong.

When the doctor has serious concerns about the possibility of glaucoma but isn't sure, he will sometimes perform a "provocative test" to "provoke" a temporary increase in eye pressure. It is not done often. The test requires that a patient's eye pressure be taken before the test begins. The patient is told to drink a great deal of water in a short period of time, then the tonometer is used again. The water overloads and overwhelms the eye's drainage system. The degree of overloading and the amount of time it takes the eye pressure to return to normal help the doctor decide if the patient actually has glaucoma.

There is also a provocative test for angle-closure glaucoma, a type of glaucoma that we will look at later in this chapter. As with the first test, it begins with the patient's eye pressure being taken and recorded. Then the patient is blindfolded and placed in a dark room with his head down on a tabletop. If a person has that specific type of glaucoma, sitting in this position for a number of minutes will cause a temporary increase in eye pressure that the doctor can quickly document.

Finally, some people simply develop a condition called ocular hypertension. They have abnormally high intraocular pressure but none of the other signs and symptoms of glaucoma, such as damage to the optic nerve or a decreasing field of vision. A person with this condition should be examined once, twice, or even three times a year, since ocular hypertension can turn into one of the four kinds of blinding glaucoma.

The Most Common Glaucoma

Open-angle, or chronic simple glaucoma, is the most frequently occurring type. It runs in families but does not hit every member of the family. Sometimes it skips one or even several generations.

It's called open angle because, although it looks as if there is no reason why the fluid cannot drain out of the eyes properly, it can't. The blockage seems to be caused by an increased resistance to the outflow of fluid within the trabecular meshwork.

Why? No one knows—yet.

We do know that it usually affects both eyes, but the rise in pressure may be greater in one eye than in the other.

A Range of Treatments

Most cases of open-angle glaucoma can be treated with eyedrops and occasionally oral medication. The latter reduces pressure by either increasing the eye's ability to drain the fluid or by decreasing the amount of fluid that is produced. The type of medication can differ from one patient to another, depending on individual considerations.

Eyedrops. The most common eyedrops used today are the beta blockers. Usually used twice a day, they are called beta blockers because they block the beta receptors of the sympathetic nervous system. First marketed in 1978, beta blockers (such as Timoptic, Betoptic, and Betagan) reduce pressure without some of the side effects produced by other glaucoma eyedrops.

They do, however, have their own set of side effects. They can make asthma and irregular heart rhythms worse in people who already have these conditions. In some cases they can even cause emotional problems such as depression.

Before the beta blockers were developed, the mainstay of glaucoma treatment for decades was a drug called pilocarpine, available as Pilocar and Isopto Carpine. Usually used four times a day, it is highly effective for decreasing the pressure by increasing the amount of fluid that can be drained from the eye.

One problem with pilocarpine is that it constricts the pupil, reducing the amount of light that enters the eyes, thus making it harder to see. The same side effect is present with other similar drugs such as carbachol, Phospholine Iodide, and demecarium bromide. As a result, many doctors will start patients out with one of the beta blockers.

One alternative though, is Pilopine, a long-acting pilocarpine gel that can be used at night and seems to cause fewer problems than the drops.

Epinephrine eyedrops, marketed as Eppy and Epifrin, and a derivative called Propine, are used once or twice a day. They reduce intraocular pressure by decreasing the amount of fluid produced. While epinephrine does not constrict the pupils, it has been associated with burning or irritation in some patients.

Oral medication. Some pills and capsules, such as Diamox, Neptazane, and Daranide, are effective in reducing eye pressure by reducing fluid production. They are used either when a patient cannot use eyedrops or when additional medication is required.

Like the eyedrops, these medications also have side effects. They have been known to cause tingling or numbness in the fingers or toes, loss of appetite, drowsiness, mental confusion, and even kidney stones. But despite their side effects, they are very useful and their benefits often outweigh their risks. After all, as unwanted and bothersome as some of those side effects might be, the question that has to be answered is this: Would you rather put up with the side effects, or would you rather go blind?

Surgery. While most glaucoma can be controlled with medication, occasionally the drugs just won't work and a patient will have to undergo surgery—either conventional surgery or laser surgery.

In terms of conventional surgery, several different "filtering operations" have been developed to deal with glaucoma. Most of these work by opening up a new drainage channel so the built-up fluid can drain out of the eye. Some work is also being done on a valve that can be surgically implanted to control the pressure (see "New Hope for Blacks with Glaucoma" on the opposite page).

New Hope for Blacks with Glaucoma

Not only do blacks develop glaucoma three times as often as whites do, and at a younger age, but they are also eight times more likely to go blind from the disease than anyone else is.

A study conducted on the small West Indies island of St. Lucia puts those figures in better focus. Of the 1,679 black island residents examined, 8.8 percent over age 30 had glaucoma. In a similar group of white people, the expected rate would be just 2 percent of all those over 40.

To further complicate the problem, blacks are also less likely to respond to conventional glaucoma treatments. But there is hope—not just for blacks, but for all those glaucoma sufferers in need of more effective treatment. It's a new drainage valve, the Molteno implant, that can be surgically implanted in the eye to control fluid buildup.

The implant was first developed by Anthony Molteno, M.D., in the late 1960s, and then revised in the 1970s. But it wasn't until the late 1980s that anyone studied effectiveness of the device among a group of black glaucoma sufferers. That study showed impressive and encouraging results.

By implanting the mechanical drain inside the eye, researchers were able to control glaucoma in 72 percent of 83 black patients, with the help of supplementary medication. Half of these patients had failed to respond to conventional surgical techniques.

But new advances in laser surgery techniques have reduced the need for conventional surgery. Now the doctor puts a special lens on the eye. Inside this lens is a mirror that reflects the laser beam onto the trabecular meshwork. The surgeon uses the laser to burn a number of microscopic laser spots on the meshwork itself.

No one knows exactly why the procedure is so effective, but it usually improves fluid drainage and reduces eye pressure by almost 25 percent in the vast majority of patients. It has also reduced the number of conventional glaucoma surgeries by between 60 and 80 percent. As an added benefit, the entire procedure takes only 15 minutes and can be performed in the doctor's office. The effects, however, may be temporary. The laser treatment may have to be repeated, or conventional surgery may be required.

Other treatments. Marijuana and alcohol have both been used experimentally to treat glaucoma. While they both do lower intraocular pressure by decreasing fluid production, they have not proved to be as effective as other medications—especially when you consider the side effects of long-term, regular usage.

Monitoring the Disease

Glaucoma patients should have their eye pressure and optic nerves rechecked every three or four months to make sure that the medication is working or, if they've had surgery, to make sure that the condition has not returned. Sometimes more frequent monitoring is necessary until the pressure has been stabilized.

The visual field also has to be regularly examined—usually once a year—because when the optic nerve is damaged, this damage shows up in the visual field test. Whether optic nerve damage is due to direct pressure on the nerve or pressure on the blood vessels that supply the nerve, the damage can usually be seen through an ophthalmoscope.

In a normal eye, the optic nerve is pink with a small indented cup in the center and a healthy-looking pink rim all around it. In an eye with uncontrolled glaucoma, however, the cup becomes wider and the rim narrower. If the pressure stays elevated, the nerve gradually turns from healthy pink to pale white. Before long, the entire rim of pink tissue disappears. The cup begins to look more like a crater on a bone white base.

While this process usually takes place slowly over a number of years, it can happen in a matter of just a few months if the eye pressure is very high.

As you might expect, the slow destruction of the optic nerve is matched by a loss of peripheral vision, which continues until total blindness occurs. It is this deterioration that is traced and tracked through the visual field examination. (The loss of central vision is also one of the signs of glaucoma—usually the last sign before total blindness—which is why doctors also test for it.)

There are several methods to test the visual field, some

more sensitive than others. In most tests, you stare at a point directly in front of your eyes. A spot of light, or some other bright object, is brought in from the side. You continue to look straight ahead and then signal when you can see the bright spot out of the corner of your eye, in your peripheral vision.

For people with normal vision, the field of vision is quite wide, extending from one side of the head to the other and from the top of the head to well below the chin. You can test your own field of vision by staring straight ahead, extending your arms, and bringing your fingers across your field of vision from one side to the other. Remember to keep staring straight ahead. Now do the same thing by bringing your fingers down in front from a point higher than your head to one well below the chin. The area where your fingers first come into view is the edge of your visual field.

Using a machine called a *perimeter*, a doctor can map your visual field on paper and compare it to earlier tests to see if there have been any changes. In addition to mapping out the limits of the visual field, the doctor can also check for blind spots within the field itself. The perimeter can quickly locate a person's normal blind spot as well as any others that shouldn't be there.

Everyone has a natural blind spot in each eye, where the optic nerve joins the retina. Any light that lands on it does not get transmitted to the brain because there are no photoreceptors (rods and cones) over the head of the nerve. The normal blind spot is usually so small that we are rarely aware of it.

If the visual field testing shows that there are other blind spots, that indicates that there is some abnormality in the retina, the optic nerve, or even the brain. The size, type, and location of blind spots, coupled with the size and shape of the visual field, are good indicators of what is happening inside the eye itself.

Prognosis: Excellent

As we've said, without treatment, open-angle glaucoma can lead to total blindness. But that can easily be prevented.

If antiglaucoma drops, pills, surgery, or laser treatments are used, the prognosis is excellent. But you have to accept the fact that if you have glaucoma and are taking medication to control it, you will probably have to take that medication for the rest of your life.

The medicine does not cure the condition. It merely gives you a day-to-day reprieve. If you stop taking it, the eye pressure will once again start to climb, and you could lose some vision. The key is to visit your doctor for testing on a regular basis to make sure that the glaucoma is kept under control.

Walk Away from Pressure Problems?

Forget what Ma Bell tells you. Let your feet do the walking, and your eyes do the seeing.

Walking and other regular exercise may reduce the odds of your developing glaucoma, according to a study by researchers at the Oregon Health Sciences University in Portland. The researchers tested the blood pressure and eye pressure of a group of 16 sedentary men and women in their early thirties to midforties. After they were put on a regular exercise program for 16 weeks, both their blood pressure and eye pressure were lower.

Does this prove that getting and keeping yourself physically fit will prevent glaucoma? No.

Does it suggest that exercise could help save your sight—as well as the rest of your body? Yes.

Other Types of Glaucoma

There are three other types of glaucoma.

Angle-closure glaucoma, also known as narrow-angle glaucoma, accounts for less than 5 percent of all glaucoma. But when it does strike, it strikes fast. It occurs when the outflow of fluid is suddenly blocked, which causes a quick fluid backup and a rapid and dangerous climb in intraocular pressure. It is an emergency condition.

A patient can experience severe eye pain, blurred vision, colored halos around lights, nausea, and vomiting. Unless the pressure is relieved within a few hours, the patient can be permanently blinded.

Open-angle glaucoma

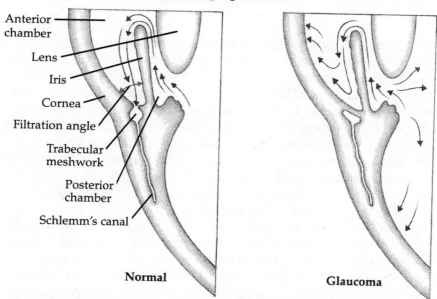

Anterior chamber
Lens
Iris
Cornea
Filtration angle
Trabecular meshwork
Posterior chamber
Schlemm's canal

Normal

Glaucoma

In open-angle glaucoma (right), the filtration angle appears normal. For reasons not really understood, there is resistance to fluid draining out of the eye. When this happens, fluid pressure builds up in the eye slowly.

Narrow-angle glaucoma

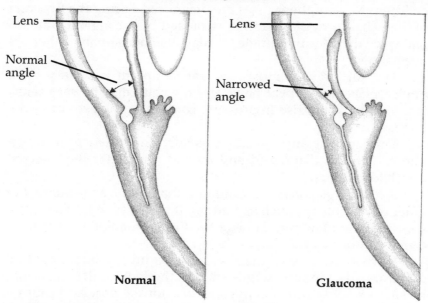

Lens

Normal angle

Lens

Narrowed angle

Normal

Glaucoma

In narrow-angle glaucoma (right), the filtration angle is anatomically narrow and can close off completely. When this happens, fluid pressure builds up in the eye suddenly.

Angle-closure glaucoma usually occurs for anatomical reasons. In certain types of eyes, the filtration angle—which is where the fluid drains out of the eye—is quite narrow, and when the lens enlarges, the angle can get crowded and blocked. This is more likely if the eye is small—a farsighted eye, for example. Its structure may be particularly crowded in the front.

Once angle-closure glaucoma has been diagnosed, it must be treated immediately. Pilocarpine drops are frequently used to constrict the pupil and lower the intraocular pressure. Oral antiglaucoma medications, such as glycerin, can also be taken.

Once the pressure has been brought under control, an operation—a peripheral iridectomy—is performed to make sure that the problem doesn't happen again. A hole is made in the outer iris and a small snip of tissue is removed, either with conventional surgery or with a laser. Because the two eyes are anatomically similar, the surgeon usually performs the operation on the opposite eye as well. The risk factor involved in the operation—which is low—is outweighed by the risk of a second serious attack of glaucoma. This is one situation where the operation generally cures glaucoma.

Congenital glaucoma is the principal form of glaucoma to hit children. Most of these cases are diagnosed during the first year of life. This form of glaucoma is caused by a congenital abnormality of the filtration angle. It may also accompany other abnormalities.

The earliest and most-constant symptom is watery eyes. The corneas may appear hazy, and the child may be very sensitive to light. If the rise in pressure continues, the eyes can even increase in size.

Congenital glaucoma must usually be treated by surgery. The earlier it is diagnosed and treated, the better the eyesight the child is left with.

Secondary glaucoma is a condition that can be a by-product of other eye problems, such as trauma. If you get hit in the eye, for example, the blow can damage the filtration angle so that fluid cannot properly drain out of the eye.

If the tissue inside the eye becomes inflamed (a condition called uveitis), the iris might stick to the lens or the trabecular meshwork. This will also prevent the normal flow and cause a buildup of pressure inside the eye.

Diabetics have special eye problems, which are dealt with in more detail in chapter 13. Secondary glaucoma may be one of them. It develops because blood vessels may grow uncontrollably over the iris and obstruct the flow of fluid through the eye. This is sometimes called neovascular glaucoma.

Secondary glaucoma can sometimes develop after surgery. Or it can be a side effect of using eyedrops containing corticosteroids. No one yet knows why steroid eyedrops cause some people to develop glaucoma, but it happens. So when they are being used, the eye pressure should be monitored carefully.

As with all the other forms of glaucoma, constant vigilance is the best protection against this stealthy thief.

CHAPTER 10

SPOTS, DOTS, AND FLOATERS
SEEING WHAT'S INSIDE YOUR EYES

Out, damned spot! out, I say!

Shakespeare, *Macbeth*

We all have our blind spots. We're born with them. It's our blind spots that let us see. Our blind spots are somewhere in the center of the retina. They are where the optic nerve goes through the back wall of the eye, carrying light-triggered electrical impulses to the brain, where we do our actual "seeing." There are no rods or cones at the point where the optic nerve goes through the eye, so there is nothing there to see with.

Sometimes, however, we have other temporary blind spots that are created by a burst of light. They block our vision for a short time. You'll usually get such a spot, called an afterimage, (see "After the Flash: A Lingering Image" on the opposite page) after you've looked at a bright light, such as a photographer's strobe light.

After the Flash: A Lingering Image

"I couldn't see a thing after the flash."

When a sudden bright light hits the eyes, the photoreceptors in the retina that registered that light go into temporary overload. For a while they won't register anything at all. Then, when they do get back to work, they are very likely to produce a reverse after-image of the light that overloaded them. It's like a photographic negative.

The most common afterimage is the one you get when you stare into a photographer's strobe light. The bright spot of strobe light turns into what appears to be an equally large spot of dark-ness—sometimes blue, sometimes green—that appears to get between your eyes and whatever you are trying to look at. The dark spot is produced by the overloaded rods and cones on the retina, which are temporarily out of service.

The same thing can happen when someone turns on a bright light in a dark room or lights a match in the dark.

If you are in the dark and know that a light is about to be turned on, you can prepare yourself for the change in lighting by closing one eye until after the light goes on. That will reduce the time spent waiting for the spot to go away. You can also partly shield your eyes with your hand so that they can slowly grow ac-customed to the light, instead of being hit with the full force of the light all at once.

The brightness of the light is only one factor in determining how long the afterimage will last. The other one is how "open" your eyes were. If your eyes were adjusted to very dim lighting—meaning the pupils were wide open to capture as much light as possible—the afterimage will last longer because more light hit the retina. If, however, you're in a brightly lit setting already, your pupils will be contracted to keep out the excess light and any af-terimage will not last as long.

Other types of spots can be created with pressure, light, or by learning how to "look" at the inside of your eyes (see "'Seeing Stars'—And Other Special Effects" on page 135).

How to Find Your Blind Spot

The normal blind spot is so small that we rarely even notice it. But it is there, and it can be mapped with a machine called a *perimeter*. If you don't happen to have a perimeter handy and you still want to find your blind spot, you can use a straight pin instead.

You do not stick the pin in anything. You look at it.

Take the pin—one with a white head works best—and hold it directly in front of you. While looking straight ahead, move the pin slowly from side to side. If you concentrate on keeping your eyes straight ahead, you will find that the head of the pin disappears briefly in a small area just to the outside of your straight-ahead central vision. Do the same thing while moving the pin up and down. If you concentrate, you may be able to map out your blind spot's horizontal and vertical dimensions.

The reason you're not usually aware of the blind spot is that the eye "fills in" the image with what surrounds it. It's kind of like ink "leaking" out of a picture in a magazine and coloring the blank space around it.

So much for our normal blind spots, the ones we were born with. As we trudge the road of our destiny, we pick up others along the way.

Those Mysterious Floaters

Sometimes we notice spots that seem to float across our field of vision, especially if we are looking at a bright background, such as a clear blue sky. These "floaters" are usually caused by bits of debris floating around in the vitreous, the jellylike substance that fills most of the eye. The ancient Romans used to call floaters *muscae volitantes*, which is Latin for "flying flies."

These "flying flies" flit between the cornea and retina, so the light entering the eye hits the spots and creates shadows on the retina itself—like a rotten tomato flying between a spotlight and the singer on stage. As we get older, the vitreous becomes more liquid and less jellylike, and the floaters become more prominent.

Floaters can also be produced when the vitreous detaches from the back of the eye. This detachment is sometimes accompanied by an occasional sensation of flashing or flickering lights and an increased number of floating spots. This on-again, off-again flickering or flashing can last for several weeks.

"Seeing Stars"— And Other Special Effects

If you close your eyes and rub them hard, you'll probably see dots, spots, and flashes and dashes of colors. These images are called phosphenes. They are produced by pressure on your eyes. Your optic nerve translates that pressure into all sorts of bizarre patterns. That's why being socked in the eye or hit on the head will make you "see stars."

While phosphenes are really physically induced hallucinations, there are a number of other things you can see on the inside of your eyeballs that actually do exist—like the blood and blood vessels inside your eyes.

If you stare at a brightly lit sheet of white paper or at a clear, bright blue sky for a while, you might see luminous points or spots of light darting around in front of you, just out of reach. Sometimes these spots appear as very bright circles with darker centers. They often appear to have tails, like comets.

While no one is absolutely certain what it is you are seeing, the general consensus is that you are watching your own blood cells moving through the capillaries in your retina.

Sometimes, if the light is right, you can actually see the blood vessels running through your retina. This might happen in a doctor's office while your eyes are being examined through a special lamp that shines a light on the back portion of the surface of the eye. The "tree branch" pattern you see corresponds to your retinal blood vessels.

In the same way that your brain "fills in" for your blind spot, it also fills in for the shadows that fall on your retina from the blood vessels inside your eye. But it only fills in for them when they fall in their normal place.

When the eyes are lit from a different angle and the shadows fall on a portion of the retina that doesn't normally "see" them, your brain actually lets you see it, too.

A vitreous detachment can look like an insect, a tree branch, or a doughnut being wagged back and forth in front of your eye. The peculiar shape is actually the ringlike attachment of the vitreous around the optic nerve. As the vitreous body contracts with age, this attachment is often pulled loose and floats inside the eye indefinitely. Sometimes it floats out of the visual axis. Sometimes it breaks up and goes away. Usually the brain adapts to its presence and we are able to ignore it.

As a rule, a vitreous detachment is nothing to worry about. Only rarely does it create a hole or tear in the retina that may cause tiny blood vessels to break and bleed. But the flashing lights it produces could be tied to a migraine—with or without the headache (see "Not All Migraines Ache" below).

If the flashing lights are accompanied by a large number of new spots, or a decrease in your vision, you may have a detached retina (see chapter 11), and you should see your ophthalmologist as soon as possible.

Not All Migraines Ache

Flashing lights that appear as jagged lines or "heat waves" in both eyes and last for about 10 or 20 minutes sometimes accompany or precede migraines. They are usually caused by a spasm and dilation of blood vessels in the brain. If they are accompanied by a headache, you have a migraine headache.

But not all migraines are accompanied by headache pain. These painless migraines are referred to as ophthalmic migraines. They may be associated with peculiar visual phenomena such as light sensations and defects in the field of vision. Doctors can't say for sure if painless migraines will lead to regular migraines or any permanent visual field loss.

If you have smaller floaters, you can even stir them up by moving your eyes around swiftly in all directions for a few seconds. This creates a "current" in the liquid inside the eye so that the floaters are moved around much like flotsam or jetsam in the ocean. After you've shaken them up, look at a plain, bright background for a while and watch as gravity "settles" the float-ers. It's a lot like one of those glass balls with a winter scene inside that is filled with liquid and plastic flakes that "snow" when you shake it.

Regardless of whether the floaters you see look like tree branches, insects, doughnut holes, or snow, they are usually just condensed pieces of vitreous or other particles that the eye cannot dispose of through the blood system. No matter how annoying they may be, they are quite harmless, which is nice, because there is nothing we can do about them.

While large floaters can persist for months—or even years—they usually do disappear eventually. If you have float-ers, the odds are that over a period of time you will get so used to them that you will literally see right through them. You will unconsciously adjust to their presence in much the same way that you have adjusted to the natural blind spot that each eye has.

Floaters might also be a symptom of an inflammation, such as uveitis (see chapter 6). In these cases, the floaters are usually clumps of white blood cells that are cast off by the choroid or ciliary body, the pigmented tissues connected to the iris.

Inflammations, like uveitis, or infections can increase the number of floaters dramatically. This may be an indication of a sight-threatening condition.

So while most floaters can be ignored, if they persist, get worse, or interfere with your vision, check with your doctor.

CHAPTER 11

RETINA PROBLEMS
GLITCHES
IN THE VIDEOTAPE

I am a camera with its shutter open, quite passive, recording, not thinking.

Christopher Isherwood,
Goodbye to Berlin, A Berlin Diary

For years the traditional explanation of the retina began: "It's the film in the camera." Today there's an even better analogy: "It's the tape in the video recorder."

Film and videotape are both used to produce the same end results—pictures. But they do so in two different ways, and the way video technology works is quite a bit closer to the way your retina works than film is. For example:

● Film is a permanent record of an image. A piece of videotape, on the other hand, can be erased and used time after time to record different images. But the videotape image can be stored electronically and re-called for later use.

- Film images are seen by shining light through the film. Videotape images are seen by electronically converting the magnetic impulses recorded on the tape into visible and recognizable patterns.
- Film does not require any electrical power. Videotape does.
- Film requires developing. Videotape does not.

Like videotape, the retina is used over and over again from the moment you are born. Even when your eyes are closed, your retina is taking pictures—of darkness.

As we saw in chapter 1, the retina is a very thin, transparent lining that covers the inside of the back of the eye like wallpaper. It contains millions of light-sensitive photoreceptor cells, called rods and cones. And yes, they're called rods and cones because that's what they're shaped like.

These rods and cones are fed by the retinal blood vessels, which share a path to the eye with the optic nerve, and another group of microscopic blood vessels in the choroid, between the retina and the sclera (the outside wall of the eye). The retina also gets necessary nutrients from a layer of tissue called the retinal pigmented epithelium.

The rods and cones contain the visual pigment rhodopsin, which has a chemical structure similar to that of vitamin A—the vitamin supplied by carrots and other good-for-your-eyes deep-yellow-colored vegetables. When light hits rhodopsin, the pigment undergoes a slight change in its molecular configuration. These changes spark electrical signals that transmit an impulse through the optic nerve to the brain in much the same way that light is transmitted from a video camera to the videotape recorder and cassette. The occipital lobes in the back of the brain function much like a video player, taking these electrical impulses and translating them back into pictures, which we then "see."

These pictures are permanently stored in the brain as electrical impulses and can be recalled via memory at any time. When you recall an image, you see it with your brain, not your eyes. People who have gone blind can still "see" images in their mind that they "recorded" before they lost their vision.

There is one more way in which the retina is like both film

and videotape. It is very delicate. But unlike either film or video-tape, the retina cannot be replaced—yet.

In experiments with rats suffering from retinitis pigmen-tosa, a condition we'll look at later in this chapter, researchers have successfully transplanted healthy cells, placing them be-neath the damaged retina in an attempt to halt the disease pro-cess. Even though the retina itself was not transplanted, medical science is now one small step closer to doing so.

Aside from retinitis pigmentosa, the main threats to the ret-ina are tears, holes, and detachments.

Torn and Detached Retinas

A tear in the retina is like a tiny rip. If the tear extends to the point that a piece of the retina hangs down from the inner surface of the eye like a torn shirt pocket hanging down from the shirt, it is called a detached retina. A hole in the retina is just that, and the piece of retina that tore out of that hole will be found floating in the vitreous.

Aging is the single most common cause of retinal tears, holes, and detachments. Nearly three-quarters of all retinal de-tachments occur between the ages of 40 and 70. As you get older, the jellylike vitreous that fills the inside of the eye can shrink. This is perfectly natural. And because the vitreous is at-tached to the retina in different spots, it can sometimes pull a piece of the retina off the inside wall of the eye while it is shrink-ing. The vitreous can also shrink due to eye inflammations or injury.

A hard blow to the eye can also damage the retina. Torn and detached retinas have forced many prizefighters and other ath-letes out of their sports, and left others blind because they wouldn't quit when they should have.

Nearsighted people are a bit more likely than other people to develop retinal tears as they get older, because their eyes are longer than normal. This stretches and thins the retina and puts extra stress on it.

In some cases the cause may be genetic. Weak and easily torn or detached retinas may run in a family.

Diseases such as diabetes and cancer, or an eye inflammation, may also cause retinal tears and detachments. Sometimes a condition like uveitis—which causes an inflammation within the vitreous—leads to debris collection or scar tissue formation inside the eye. Debris or scar tissue can adhere to the retina and tear a hole in it.

Any tug on the retina can also rupture tiny blood vessels, which will then bleed inside the eye, adding to the problem. And once the tear or hole has started, fluid that is filtered out of the vitreous body can seep through the opening, building up behind the retina like a blister. The blister almost always gets bigger. This forces more of the retina to detach from the eye, like paint blistering off a wall.

Watching For Symptoms

There are different sets of symptoms for different retinal problems. When the initial tear occurs, you will see light flashes and floaters (spots), cobwebs, dots, or squiggly lines. Usually these symptons develop with trachon or pulling on the retina, and no detachment occurs.

Once part of the retina actually detaches from the surface of the eye, part of your vision grows dim. What you will see are shadows, blurs, clouds, veils, or dark areas. The classic description of a retinal detachment compares it to having a veil or curtain hanging over the field of vision.

If the retina is detached along the outer edges or bottom of the eye, your peripheral vision is damaged. But if the detachment spreads to the center of the back of the eye—to the macula, which controls the sharpest part of your central vision—the vision loss can be much more dramatic and potentially more serious.

Prompt surgery is the only way to correct a retinal detachment. The sooner it is performed, the better the chances of recovering lost vision.

Finding—and Reaching— the Problem

The first thing a surgeon must do before beginning to reattach a detached retina or repair any other retinal hole or tear is determine exactly where the problem is. An *indirect ophthalmoscope* is used to look inside the eye, through the pupil, and to carefully chart the precise location of the tear or hole. The doctor continues to check the inside of the eye regularly throughout the procedure.

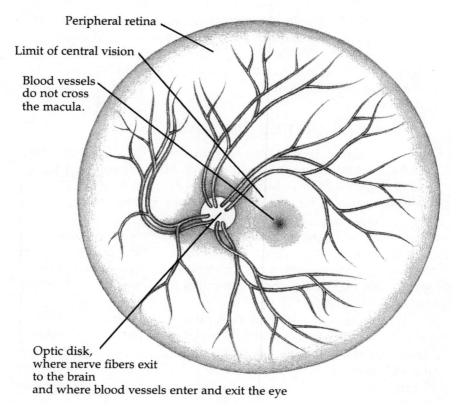

Peripheral retina

Limit of central vision

Blood vessels
do not cross
the macula.

Optic disk,
where nerve fibers exit
to the brain
and where blood vessels enter and exit the eye

This is the doctor's view of the retina and the blood vessels that run through it as seen through an ophthalmoscope. The small, central dark portion of the retina is the macula, responsible for central vision. The rest of the retina is responsible for peripheral vision. The circle represents the optic nerve.

Once the problem has been pinpointed, the next step is to get at it. Because the retina covers much of the back half of the inside of the eye—directly opposite the cornea—only the forward edges are easy to get to. Luckily, most holes or tears in the retina appear around those edges. Actually, the doctor has to get behind the exact spot where the retina has been torn or detached. The operation is performed on the outside of the eyeball, not the inside. That means gaining access to the back of the eye. The only way to get at the back is by coming in through the side. So the farther back the tear, the harder it is to get at.

This is how the surgeon does it.

First the eyelids are pulled open as far as possible. Then the surgeon isolates the muscles of the eye, the ones that control its movement. They are like cables coming out of the sides of the eyeball. Sutures are tied around each muscle. The surgeon uses those sutures like ropes to pull up, down, sideways, whatever it takes to get the eye into the best possible position for the operation.

Upside-Down Surgery

Surgical techniques have evolved over the years. While some look quite normal in an operating room, others look as though they belong in an auto-repair garage.

Today when someone has a major retinal detachment and there is a large piece of the retina hanging down, an air bubble or certain types of gas or oil may be injected directly into the eye to push the retina into position so that it can be "welded" back into place.

Some years ago, however, surgeons achieved the same result by having the patient lie facedown so gravity would help the flap fall back into place on its own. Then, once the flap was in place, they would operate from underneath.

The technique required a special operating table that held the patient suspended above the surgeon in much the same way that a hoist lifts a car so that a mechanic can work from below.

Making Minor Repairs

Approximately one of every ten Americans will develop a simple hole or tear that can be repaired in the doctor's office in a matter of minutes.

If there is no fluid beneath the tear and the retina has not yet detached itself from the eye's inner surface, the tear can be sealed off, or "spot welded," relatively simply with either a freezing treatment or an argon laser beam.

No matter which method the surgeon uses, the purpose is the same—to create scar tissue. Scar tissue produces strong connections, functioning like a reinforced seam on a pair of pants. It can withstand extra pressure without ripping.

Freezing—a process known as cryotherapy or cryopexy—is accomplished with a probe placed directly behind the tear. The point of the probe, with a temperature of −80°C (−113°F), instantly freezes the spot on the surface of the sclera where it touches. It forms scar tissue on both the outside and the inside of the eye and seals the torn retina to prevent further tearing. This procedure can sometimes be done on an outpatient basis with a local anesthetic to numb the eye.

Laser photocoagulation accomplishes the same thing as freezing, but it does so with heat instead of cold. It too can be done on an outpatient basis. With this method, the laser is aimed through the patient's pupil, allowing the doctor to work from the front of the eye instead of through the back.

Once the hole or tear has been sealed off, a *scleral buckle* is often inserted to relieve the traction that caused the tear in the first place. (This can be done only in an operating room; it cannot be done in the doctor's office.) First a tiny belt is placed around the eye, under the muscles and behind the lids where it cannot be seen or felt. The belt goes around the eye from top to bottom and holds a piece of silicon or sponge in place over the torn area. This is a permanent girdle for the eye.

The pressure of the belt and buckle forms a slight protective indentation in the surface of the eye directly over the tear. It's like gently pressing your thumb into a balloon, and it relieves the vitreous trachon on the retina. Fortunately, the buckle usually does not change the shape of the eye enough to cause any change in vision.

Another repair technique that is occasionally used involves an actual balloon. The surgeon first "welds" the tear shut with a freezing probe. Then the balloon, attached to a catheter, is inserted inside the eye socket, behind the tear. Once in position, the balloon is inflated until it pushes the wall of the eye against the retina and forces out the fluid that has collected there. Once this fluid has been absorbed back into the vitreous, usually after four or five days, the balloon is deflated and removed.

Yet another repair technique uses a gas bubble instead of a balloon. If the tear is located along the top or the side of the retina, some surgeons inject a gas bubble directly inside the eye. The bubble will rise up to the tear and hold it in place while it is "welded" with either a laser or a freezing probe.

Laser Treatment—Let There Be Light

Lasers are amplified beams of light that can be used to burn through solid steel or repair almost microscopic tears on the delicate retina.

The type of laser used varies with the job that is to be performed. The laser discussed here is much better on eyes than on stainless-steel doors. It is an argon laser, and it can be used in a doctor's office. It's utilized because the bright blue beam passes through the fluids of the eye without being absorbed.

Before that laser is used, eyedrops are put in the patient's eye to dilate, or open, the pupil. That way the doctor can have a good view through the pupil to the retina.

Next a drop of anesthetic is put on the eye, and the patient is then seated in front of the laser machine in a dimly lit room.

A special focusing lens, like a contact lens, is placed on the eye. This is as painless as having a normal contact lens inserted. It helps the doctor focus the laser beam on the specific parts of the retina that need to be fused.

During the actual treatment, the patient will see flashes of green light. The feeling is only rarely uncomfortable.

An important thing to remember about laser treatments is that they are designed to preserve your current vision by halting the spread of a retinal tear or other problem. Do not assume that treatment will actually improve your vision. Improvement can and will occur in some cases, but because each case is different, only your doctor can tell you what to expect.

Some patients who have been treated this way can actually see the bubble for a week or so before it dissipates and is absorbed into the system. Some surgeons believe that this technique gives the patient a better chance of recovering lost vision because there is little trauma to the eye and the eye is not deformed as it is with a scleral buckle. Furthermore, the gas bubble procedure can be done entirely in the doctor's office.

Regardless of the repair procedure used, if any fluid has leaked beneath the retina from the vitreous body and formed a blister, it must be gotten rid of before it makes the detachment worse.

Once such a fluid pocket is located, a tiny needle is inserted through the wall of the eye into the pocket. The surgeon watches the inside of the eye with an ophthalmoscope to make sure that all the fluid that has collected is drained out. In some ways it's like getting a bubble out of wallpaper.

Reattaching the Retina

The surgeon also watches to make sure that the torn flap of retina lies flat after the fluid is removed.

If draining the fluid doesn't flatten the retina, the surgeon may insert a needle in a different spot and drain more fluid. Conversely, fluid or gas can be injected to push the retina back into position. The freezing or laser treatment that was applied earlier helps the retina stay in place.

Reattaching a retina can take between 1 and 3 hours, and depending on your situation and your surgeon, may involve a combination of techniques and procedures.

Sometimes a retinal detachment occurs because the vitreous becomes heavily scarred and pulls on the retina. Or a hemorrhage inside the eye can have the same traction-creating effect. Standard reattachment procedures are useless in such cases because the vitreous would just pull the retina off the surface of the eye again once the operation was over.

To prevent that, a surgeon may perform a vitrectomy to remove the damaged vitreous body itself before reattaching the retina.

In this procedure, the surgeon actually operates inside the

eye. Working through incisions in the sides of the eye, the surgeon inserts a small surgical instrument, which functions a bit like a Roto-Rooter used to unclog drains and pipes. It chops and gobbles up the scar tissue or blood clot that was pulling on the retina. Once this traction is broken and the diseased vitreous is removed, the surgeon can reattach the retina in the normal way.

One problem with this procedure is that the conditions that caused the initial scarring or hemorrhaging can cause it to happen again once the vitreous has re-formed.

Living with the Results

Thanks to new procedures and increased expertise and knowledge, retinas can be reattached in 90 percent of all cases. If the retina cannot be reattached, it's usually because scar tissue inside the eye has created permanent wrinkles or folds in the retina itself.

While 90 percent of all retinas can be reattached, this does not mean that 90 percent of all the patients operated on will regain good vision. If the retina has been detached for several days, the retinal cells may have deteriorated to the point that perfect vision cannot be restored. So the more quickly the retina is reattached, the better the chances for good vision. No matter how successful the surgery is, though, any spot where the retina has been welded to the sclera becomes a blind spot. But because most tears and holes occur in the peripheral retina, these blind spots are usually not noticeable.

As a rule, one-third of all patients who have their retinas reattached see well after the surgery. Another third have moderately good vision that can sometimes be helped by new glasses or low-vision aids. The rest have to settle for considerably less.

Regardless of the results of your surgery—good or bad—you should continue to have your eyes checked on a regular basis, at least once a year. The physical conditions that caused the first detachment could cause you more trouble later on. And there is a chance that the same problem will develop in your other eye. If that does happen, and if you catch it early, your odds for preserving good vision in the second eye are much, much higher.

Retinitis Pigmentosa

Actually a group of degenerative retinal diseases, retinitis pigmentosa (RP) is characterized by a loss of peripheral vision and night blindness (difficulty seeing in dim light or at night). Approximately 60 percent of all people with RP inherit the condition. By working with family medical histories, it is possible for an eye doctor to construct a family tree of those people most likely to have RP.

Although RP is an eye disease, approximately 10 percent of RP sufferers also suffer from either partial or complete deafness. No one really knows why.

The word *retinitis* was a poor choice for the disease's name, because the suffix -*itis* in medical words usually refers to an inflammation. But the retina is not inflamed in RP. Instead, it is degenerating.

For reasons not yet understood, the photoreceptors in the eyes—the rods and cones—degenerate and lose their ability to transmit electrical signals to the brain. With no electrical signals to interpret, the brain has nothing to "see."

The word *pigmentosa* refers to the small specks of black pigment seen in or on the retina. These black specks are produced by the retinal pigmented epithelium (RPE), a layer of tissue directly beneath the retina. The presence of such specks does not always mean that the patient has RP, because the release of pigment specks also occurs in other diseases.

As a rule, the disease hits the peripheral vision first and is referred to as peripheral retinal degeneration. As the retina slowly continues to degenerate, the patient is left with only tunnel vision. In some cases the degeneration continues until the patient goes completely blind.

As the rods and cones within the retina degenerate, the patient also develops night blindness. And 40 percent of RP sufferers also develop cataracts. Although these cataracts are usually small, sometimes they do interfere with what vision remains.

There is a certain degree of controversy surrounding cataract surgery for RP patients. If the RP has destroyed much of the macula—which provides central vision—the benefits of even a successful cataract operation might be minimal at best.

Treatments Are Limited

There is no cure for retinitis pigmentosa.

Research centers around the world are deeply involved in RP research, and while progress is being made in understanding the disease, there is still no clear indication that a cure is on the horizon.

A small—very small—number of RP sufferers can be helped by taking vitamin A. Vitamin E therapy may also be helpful, but it should be discussed with a doctor first.

Vitamins A and E were first tried because RP is sometimes associated with a number of lipid disorders, in which the body is unable to process certain fats. Taking the vitamins has slowed down or even stopped the spread of RP in some cases. But for most patients, the vitamins have had no effect at all. If you want to try vitamin therapy, talk it over with your doctor first.

Aside from those rare cases where vitamins A and E do work, all a doctor can do for RP sufferers is record the disease's progress and recommend certain visual aids that may help slow down the disease or at least let the patients better utilize what vision they have left.

There is scientific evidence that UV light can damage the retina, and UV coatings, screens, or filters on eyeglasses or sunglasses seem to have slowed the disease's progress in some instances. Low-vision aids such as magnifying lenses; flashlights with wide, strong fields; and hand-held night-vision aids that change infrared light into visible light might also help (see chapter 16).

Solar Retinopathy

Back around 400 B.C., when the world was a much younger piece of real estate, Socrates warned people not to look directly into the sun during an eclipse, lest they go blind. Even then the effects of solar radiation were well known.

It wasn't until the Middle Ages, however, that anyone recorded a medical description of the blind spot in a person's visual field caused by a solar burn. The damage is done when the solar radiation hits the macula, the center of the retina, and permanently destroys the central vision.

An eclipse reduces the intensity of the sunlight, and it's the intensity that normally makes us look away. But while the brightness is reduced to a more comfortable level during an eclipse, the ultraviolet light rays thrown off by the sun are still dangerous and damaging. It's the UV radiation that can blind you.

Even though we've all been warned not to stare directly into the sun during an eclipse (or at any other time), some people— usually people on drugs, but sometimes children who don't know any better—insist on doing it. There was a rash of solar maculopathy cases—burned-out eyes—during the 1960s among people who took LSD and stared into the sun.

If you really want to watch an eclipse, never look directly at the sun. No sunglasses or filters will protect you. They provide you with only a false sense of security—not protection.

One safe way to watch an eclipse is indirectly, using the pinhole projection method that we were all told about in grade school. Keep your back to the sun and watch it that way.

But the safest way to watch an eclipse is at night—on the 11 o'clock news.

Retinopathy of Prematurity

Sometimes a cure for one tragic condition creates another one. Retinopathy of prematurity is a case in point.

It is a condition that strikes babies who are born prematurely. Because they are so frail and underdeveloped when they are born, additional oxygen must be added to the atmosphere inside the incubator to keep them alive.

But the extra oxygen they need to keep them alive can also blind them by stimulating the growth of their retinal blood vessels. Those vessels can grow wildly inside the eye, causing the retina to scar and hemorrhage.

For years, doctors and researchers believed that the blindness associated with prematurity occurred because the babies were exposed to too much light. Thus many premature infants were kept blindfolded, but they still went blind. It wasn't until the late 1940s that researchers began to realize that oxygen was the problem. When doctors started reducing the oxygen content in the incubators, the rate of blindness went down.

The problem couldn't be eliminated entirely, though, because premature babies still need a higher-than-normal concentration of oxygen to survive. And oxygen might not be the only factor involved. The original researchers who thought that light was responsible might also be partly right.

Current research indicates that excessive light might have the same effect on a premature baby that excessive oxygen does. Incubators are kept well lighted so that a baby's progress—including any changes in coloration—can be more easily monitored.

Some hospitals are now covering premature babies' eyes and using tinted glass in the incubators, as well as carefully monitoring the amount of oxygen the infants receive.

Whatever the ultimate cause or causes, the unchecked and wild blood vessel development is similar to what can happen to diabetics who develop diabetic retinopathy (see chapter 13). Some researchers think that the two conditions are so similar that when progress is made in treating one condition, it will benefit victims of the other as well.

No matter what the cause, however, scars form inside the eye. As the scar tissue contracts, it pulls on the retina and detaches it from the eye's inside surface. Doctors have tried reattaching the infants' retinas, but success is rare because the retinas simply detach again as the eyes grow.

There is currently a great deal of research interest in retinopathy of prematurity because more and more premature babies are being kept alive in earlier stages of development. In order for that to be done, however, premature babies must spend more time breathing higher concentrations of oxygen.

In the United States alone, approximately 37,000 babies are born every year who weigh 3.3 pounds or less. Of these, approximately 8,000 develop some form of retinopathy of prematurity and suffer some retinal damage and vision loss. Roughly 500 of these babies will go blind.

There is no cure for retinopathy of prematurity, but some research is being done with vitamin E therapy. Tests have shown that it does interfere with the proliferation of blood vessels in the retinas of kittens. Will it work in humans? No one knows for sure—yet.

CHAPTER 12

MACULAR DEGENERATION A CENTRAL THREAT TO SIGHT

First senior citizen: "My eyes sure aren't what they were 50 years ago."
Second senior citizen: "What is?"

Macular degeneration is one of the chief causes of vision loss among elderly people.

There is no cure. But there are treatments and techniques that just might halt some forms of the disease in some cases and delay it in others. There are also ways to help improve whatever vision is left after the disease strikes.

As its name indicates, macular degeneration is a disease in which the macula—the central portion of the retina—degenerates. It is the macula that lets you read, drive, and distinguish detail. Without it, you couldn't see the world around you at night, or even what's right in front of you during the day.

While the macula consists of only 10 percent of the entire surface of the retina, that 10 percent provides you with a lot more important sight than all the rest combined. Whereas a person who suffers from tunnel vision can at least see straight ahead and read and recognize fine detail, a person suffering

152

from severe macular degeneration can see only the "sides" of the tunnel—nothing right in front of the eyes.

We know what happens to people with macular degeneration, especially to those suffering from it in its most common form, age-related macular degeneration (AMD). What we're not sure of is why it happens.

We do know that the problem very likely starts in Bruch's membrane, a cellophanelike piece of tissue that separates the retina from the blood vessels of the choroid. This membrane regulates the transfer of oxygen and nutrients from the blood vessels to the retina.

For reasons still not understood, something often goes wrong with the membrane in people over age 50, and it loses its ability to function properly. Although there is no apparent connection between AMD and cataracts, except that both conditions happen to strike elderly eyes, there are indications that blocking out ultraviolet light might actually reduce the severity of both conditions.

There is evidence also of a possible link between AMD and hardening of the arteries. The blood vessels in your eyes can harden and get blocked up just like the veins and arteries in the rest of your body. Loss of blood flow to the retina can mean a loss of necessary nourishment.

Researchers are also finding indications that nutrition might be involved.

Studies suggest—not prove, just suggest—that taking oral zinc supplements may retard the vision loss caused by one type of AMD—dry AMD, which will be discussed later in this chapter. Some studies have shown that taking 100 milligrams of zinc twice a day may slow down the degeneration.

It is virtually impossible to develop a conclusive testing procedure, since AMD varies from person to person. Some people never go blind, while others go blind within a matter of months. In any event, zinc does appear to help some people.

Zinc is an essential nutrient that plays an important role in a number of metabolic processes in the body, including several within the retina. Side effects—including anemia and gastric ulcers—can occur with high doses, however. As a rule, those who were given 200 milligrams a day in these studies reported nothing worse than an upset stomach. At that dosage, zinc can irritate the stomach lining, much as aspirin does. Check with your doctor first before taking supplemental zinc at these levels.

Finally, one cause of macular dysfunction that can—and does—strike people of all ages is diabetes mellitus. This and other diabetes-related eye problems are dealt with in chapter 13.

Know the Warning Signs

The first indications of potential macular problems are scattered white and yellow spots called drusen, which appear within the macula. They are a bit like liver or age spots. You can't see them, but your eye doctor can.

No one is sure exactly what these spots are, but current research suggests that they are very likely accumulations of waste material produced by the retina that cannot be eliminated, possibly because of problems with Bruch's membrane.

Approximately one-third of all people over age 50 will develop drusen. While they very rarely disturb a person's vision, they do serve as a warning that the eye is predisposed to developing macular problems. All told, approximately 20 million elderly Americans have drusen. And every year about 100,000 people with drusen develop other macular problems.

The most common symptoms that the patient can recognize are blurred vision and increased difficulty in seeing details—near and/or far—even when corrective lenses are worn. Shapes and contours may also look distorted and even shimmer as you look at them. Bright colors may look dull, and blind spots—macular scotomata—may appear in the center of your visual field. The size or color of an object might look different depending on which eye you are looking at it with.

A "Flip-Up" Tip for Better Vision

Most elderly people have a problem adjusting quickly from bright light to dim light, and vice versa. This can sometimes be an indication that they are developing macular degeneration.

One way to make living with the problem a little easier is to use flip-up or clip-on sunglasses that can be put on or taken off quickly, such as when driving from a shadowy lane to a sunny street—or back again.

Because macular degeneration sometimes affects only one eye, some people are not aware that they have it because their good eye compensates for it. They can still read, thread a needle, drive a car, and see details.

Three Types of Trouble

There are three distinct types of age-related macular degeneration. The extent of your visual loss, and your prospects for treatment, will depend on which form of the disease you develop.

Dry Macular Degeneration

The most common problem is the simple degeneration, atrophy, and death of the rods and cones—the photoreceptors—within the macular region of the retina. This is called dry, or atrophic, macular degeneration. It accounts for between 85 and 90 percent of all cases.

The degeneration usually takes place slowly, and only rarely does it completely destroy the macula. Some central vision usually remains, and most victims are able to read with the help of a magnifying glass or other low-vision aid. While reading may be frustrating, at least it is still possible.

Even when AMD does take out the entire macula, patients can usually still get around independently. They can't drive, but they can walk. They even can watch movies or TV by looking out of the corners of their eyes.

Researchers have also developed an "intraocular telescope," which can be implanted in the eyes of some people with AMD (see "Don't Overlook Low-Vision Aids" on page 156).

Although doctors can chart, record, document, and even photograph the progress of dry macular degeneration, they cannot do anything to stop it or even slow it down. The degeneration is happening inside the retina itself, and a successful retina transplant is still—at best—only a theoretical possibility.

One additional problem with dry AMD is that people suffering from it can also develop wet AMD at the same time.

Don't Overlook Low-Vision Aids

Low-vision aids such as magnifying lenses and other devices can help you live with macular degeneration. They can make the difference between being able to read and not being able to read. It's that simple—and important. But too often doctors ignore these aids or fail to stress how much they can do for their patients.

Some low-vision aids are simply hand-held magnifiers with lights in them. Some attach to glasses. Some even project reading material onto a television screen.

One of the newest and most exciting aids is an *intraocular telescope*, which can be implanted in the eyes. Although they are still in the experimental stages, there have been some successes with these implants since they were first developed in the early 1980s at New York's Columbia University.

They are not for all AMD patients. Potential recipients must have some central vision left. They must also have the disease in both eyes, because the implant will magnify the image they see. If they still had one "good" eye, the different sizes of the images each eye would send to the brain would cause double vision.

Like a telescope, the implanted lens magnifies what the person sees to such an extent that it can actually improve central vision. But while it improves central vision, it can reduce peripheral vision—unless a special pair of prescription glasses is worn to compensate.

Lens implants do not cure AMD, but they can make it easier to live with.

Wet Macular Degeneration

Wet macular degeneration hits about 10 percent of all people with AMD. It is usually faster and more destructive than the dry type. But sometimes it is treatable, if it is caught early.

Wet AMD produces a sudden growth of new but abnormal blood vessels within the macula itself. They produce scars that can quickly destroy the macula to a point where even reading is impossible.

These new blood vessels grow out of the choroidal vessels, the blood vessels beneath the retina. This condition is formally called subretinal neovascularization (SRNV).

When these new blood vessels start to form, they can leak fluid and blood, which collect within the retina itself. Aside from blocking vision, the fluid also blisters the retina away from the wall of the eye and causes vision distortion. Straight lines appear to be bent and curved.

If the leaking blood vessels can be spotted soon enough—within days of appearing—they can sometimes be zapped with a laser and closed off. The important word here is *sometimes*.

Much depends on exactly where the bleeding is. If it is right over the macula, the laser will destroy the macula and your central vision as it closes off the leaking blood vessel. The treatment works only when the leaking vessels are around the periphery of the macula.

It is important to remember that the laser destroys any portion of the retina or macula that it touches. The gray spot that a person with wet AMD often sees will turn black after laser treatment. It becomes a permanent blind spot or scotoma. That part of the visual field was sacrificed to help prevent AMD from spreading throughout the rest of the macula.

Another important point to keep in mind about laser treatment for wet AMD is that it rarely actually improves your vision. As a rule, the best it can do is decrease the distortion caused by the buildup of abnormal blood vessels beneath the retina.

A Rare but Real Threat to Children

Although macular degeneration usually hits older people, there are hereditary forms of the disease that can strike at any time in a person's life. While rare, it can happen—from infancy on up.

If any of your children are suffering any vision loss, or if there is a history of macular degeneration in your family, let your eye doctor know about it. Although laser surgery has not proved effective in treating juvenile macular degeneration, low-vision aids have proved helpful.

It is also reassurring to know that children who develop the disease rarely lose all of their sight.

Not only does the treatment itself have drawbacks, but complications also can develop. The same heat that normally seals off blood vessels can cause further bleeding instead. The heat can also damage nerve cells within the macula itself, leading to an even greater vision loss.

If the eye surgeon thinks that the blood vessels can be closed off, the procedure can be done in the doctor's office. It takes about 15 minutes.

All in all, research shows that without laser treatments 60 percent of all people suffering from wet AMD suffer a noticeable loss of vision. Laser treatment reduces that number to 25 percent. Remember, however, that laser treatment does nothing for dry AMD, the most common type of macular degeneration.

Before a laser is used, the doctor conducts a test called *fluorescein angiography.* In this procedure, dye injected into the arm travels throughout the bloodstream, including the blood vessels

A Grid That Graphs Vision Loss

An *Amsler grid* looks a lot like an ordinary square sheet of graph paper with a dot right in the center. This graph has a special purpose: It can detect early signs of macular degeneration.

Developed by Swiss ophthalmologist Marc Amsler, the original grid was a 10-inch square. Today it is available from many ophthalmologists in a smaller and more convenient credit-card size.

To use it, all you have to do is look at the center dot and keep looking at it as you see the grid in your peripheral vision.

Look at the grid once a day. First block one eye and do it, then do it again with the other eye. If the lines look straight and parallel, there's nothing to worry about. But if the lines look curved or distorted or if parts of the grid are missing, either while turning the grid or while holding it still, call your doctor.

If you have already had laser treatment, you may be asked to draw a large X on the grid. Laser treatment leaves you with a blind spot, and using the X-grid, you can locate that blind spot, or scotoma, and trace it on the grid itself.

If you use a new grid sheet every week and a different color pen or pencil every day to trace the blind spot, you will quickly learn if the spot has grown or changed in any way. If it has, you should see your doctor immediately, and take along the marked grids to show exactly how your vision has changed.

in the eye. Using specialized camera equipment, the doctor then takes a series of photographs of the retina. If the doctor decides that laser treatments might help, these photographs will be used as a sort of road map during the treatment.

Since a fluorescein angiography is a photographic process—and not a type of x-ray—there is no dangerous radiation to worry about.

Once a person develops wet AMD in one eye, he is likely to develop it in the other eye, too. Even when it is "cured" or halted with laser surgery, there is a 50 percent chance that new blood vessels will form again within two years.

If new vessels do form, and if they form in the same place and can be caught soon enough, they can be zapped again with the laser. That's why many doctors supply their patients with an Amsler grid (see "A Grid That Graphs Vision Loss" below) to help them test themselves every day for further problems.

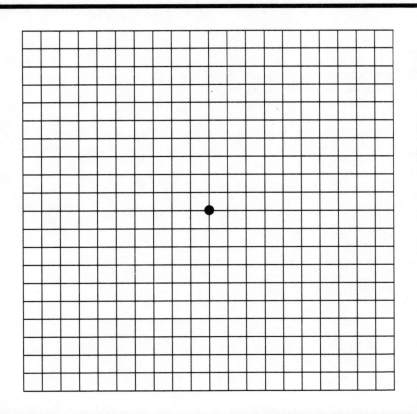

Pigmented Epithelial Detachment

The third form of AMD, pigmented epithelial detachment (PED), occurs in fewer than 5 percent of AMD cases. A person with PED has a blister beneath the macula, which causes blurring or distortion.

Laser treatment is not usually recommended for PED sufferers unless they also have abnormal blood vessel growth beneath the retina. About the only thing a doctor can do for PED is monitor it.

As with all the other forms of macular degeneration, much more research is needed before doctors can hope to truly control or reverse this vision-robbing process.

CHAPTER 13

DIABETIC EYES
AT SPECIAL RISK

Every sweet has its sour, every evil its good

Ralph Waldo Emerson

There's nothing at all sweet about the "sugar disease."

A few generations ago, people didn't associate diabetes mellitus with blindness because few people with the disease lived long enough to go blind. Today, however, when medical treatment allows most diabetics to live a normal life span, we realize that diabetes can lead to diabetic retinopathy, the leading cause of new blindness for people over the age of 20 in North America. According to the U.S. Department of Health and Human Services, people with diabetes are 29 times more likely to go blind than those without diabetes. And that's a lot of potential victims: It's estimated that there are approximately 11 million diabetics in the United States alone. That's the bad news. The good news is that if diabetic retinopathy is caught in time, it can often be stopped.

There are two types of diabetes: diabetes insipidus, which

stems from a problem with the pituitary gland, and diabetes mellitus, which is the more common and more dangerous form. Although the two diseases are unrelated, two of the symptoms are the same for both. People with either are excessively thirsty and urinate a lot.

We will be dealing with diabetes mellitus in this chapter because it is the one that can lead to eye problems. People with this condition have trouble using and storing blood sugar or glucose. Typically they have elevated blood sugar levels, and their blood vessels undergo harmful changes as a result.

Although no one is sure what causes diabetes mellitus, there are indications that it is linked to problems that develop when a person's pancreas fails to produce enough insulin, or when the body fails to use the insulin properly. Insulin is a natural hormone that the body depends on to utilize carbohydrates.

A lack of insulin will cause a buildup of sugar in the bloodstream. This excess is excreted through the urinary tract.

Diabetes mellitus is usually divided into two types: non-insulin-dependent diabetes and insulin-dependent diabetes. The first type is considered less severe. It can often be controlled with the right diet and proper lifestyle. Exercising, maintaining proper weight, and cutting down on sugar can all help.

As the name implies, people with insulin-dependent diabetes mellitus usually require insulin. The type of insulin and dosage varies from person to person. Today it is not uncommon to develop either kind of diabetes well after age 20.

Taking Aim at the Eyes

The effect that diabetes has on the sufferer's blood vessels also varies from individual to individual. Diabetic retinopathy occurs when the blood vessels that feed the retina begin to deteriorate. Once damaged by the disease, these blood vessels may leak blood or other fluid. They might become enlarged. They might even develop fragile, brushlike branches. Or all three might happen.

The disease seems to effect the eyes in another way too: There is a slightly higher incidence of cataracts in people with diabetes. Diabetics can also expect to wait a little longer for their eyes to heal after cataract surgery.

Although no one can predict what exactly will happen—or if the problems the disease causes will be major or minor—doctors know that the longer you have diabetes, the more likely you are to have diabetic retinopathy.

According to the American Academy of Ophthalmology, about 50 percent of all people who have had diabetes for more than 10 years have some blood vessel damage in their eyes. The odds of developing diabetic retinopathy increase the longer you live. After 20 years with diabetes, the likelihood is over 90 percent. Obviously, diabetic retinopathy is a major problem for those who become diabetic as children.

It is often said that diabetics who keep their blood sugar levels under control are less likely to develop eye problems than those who can't seem to get them in line. But we aren't sure if that's true, and if it is, why.

But we do know that diabetic retinopathy is very likely to hit the so-called brittle diabetics—those whose blood sugar is hard to regulate with the proper amount of insulin and who are prone to all the other related afflictions such as ulcers on the feet, kidney problems, and diabetic coma.

The Two Forms of Retinopathy

Luckily, not all people with diabetic retinopathy advance to the more serious stage of blindness. Most of the eye problems they do develop are the result of background retinopathy, the first of two stages of the disease.

Background Retinopathy

Background retinopathy is a mild form of diabetic retinopathy. Luckily, it does not cause a major loss of vision, and in about 80 percent of cases it does not progress to a more severe type of retinopathy.

In background retinopathy, vision can dim or blur because the tiny blood vessels within the eye begin to change. Some vessels close off. Some shrink. Some enlarge and form balloonlike sacs that collect blood and obstruct normal blood flow. Some leak either blood or other fluid, forming deposits, called exudates, on the surface of the retina itself or producing swelling within the retina. The blood vessels can also develop microaneurysms, tiny outpouchings of the blood vessel wall, which look like tiny dots of blood just sitting on the surface of the retina.

Sometimes these dots and exudates disappear or change locations on their own. Sometimes they don't.

The damage that background retinopathy can do is usually determined by how much leakage there is, where it collects, and how long it stays there without treatment. The damage can be much worse if the leaking blood vessels affect the macula, the central portion of the retina that provides central vision. The macula lets us see fine details, as well as all the things that are directly in front of us. If much of the macula is blocked, you could lose your ability to read, drive, or do close work.

Proliferative Retinopathy

Proliferative retinopathy is like background retinopathy, only worse—in some cases, much, much worse.

In the advanced or proliferative stage, new blood vessels can grow inside the eye. Some may grow over the surface of the retina itself or grow on the iris and cause a form of glaucoma.

Large pockets of leaking fluid or blood can collect in the vitreous, the jellylike material inside the eye, blocking or distorting the retina's view of the outside world.

Sometimes the fluid is reabsorbed naturally into the body and the vitreous clears on its own. In other cases, however, surgery is required.

Diagnosing the Problem

An ophthalmologist is the best person to tell you if you have either background or proliferative retinopathy. Some cases of background retinopathy are so mild—at first—that you might not even be aware that you have a problem. Because retinopathy can get worse, diabetics should have their eyes checked by an ophthalmologist regularly.

Your ophthalmologist will first examine the interior of your eyes with an ophthalmoscope. The doctor might also photograph the interior of the eye for more careful study. Many doctors keep a regular file of eye photographs so they can see how the patient's eye changes over time.

If there are indications that you might have diabetic retinopathy, the doctor will perform a fluorescein angiography. In this test, a dye is injected into your arm so that it will travel throughout the bloodstream, including the blood vessels in the eye.

A series of rapid photographs are taken as the dye passes through the blood vessels of the retina and choroid. This test can not only confirm the presence of retinopathy, it also shows exactly how far it has progressed. By the way, a fluorescein angiogram is a photographic process, not an x-ray, so there is no radiation to worry about.

What about Treatment?

One of the best things diabetics can do for their eyes is take care of the rest of their body by following the proper diet, maintaining correct weight, and taking any prescribed medication. They should carefully follow their physician's advice, especially in regard to exercise. Diabetics with background retinopathy should have few problems with exercising. But those with proliferative retinopathy should exercise with moderation and caution and avoid straining or leaning over with the head down.

Usually, background retinopathy doesn't require treatment. It's only when it crosses the line and becomes proliferative that anything can—or should—be done. But in all cases it is best to consult your doctor in identifying and treating problems.

There are two treatments for proliferative retinopathy. The primary and most effective treatment for proliferative retinopathy is a laser treatment called panretinal photocoagulation. It cannot, however, be used in all cases. If, for example, the damaged blood vessels are over the macula, treating the macula with the laser could destroy it. But the laser can be used successfully in many other cases.

Despite the heat that the laser generates, the treatment is

usually painless. The procedure is similar to the one used for glaucoma. The same argon laser is used. For glaucoma, it's aimed at the trabecular meshwork. For proliferative retinopathy it is aimed at the problem blood vessels.

Why does the laser work? Doctors don't know exactly. But we can make some educated guesses.

One theory is that burning and cauterizing the defective blood vessels redirects or changes the pattern of blood flow in the retina back to normal. Another theory states that, with retinopathy, there may be a relative lack of blood supply to the retina. By killing off some of the tissue, the laser reduces the amount of blood flow that the retina needs, so that demand and supply more closely match. Whichever theory ultimately proves correct, the important thing is that panretinal photocoagulation almost always works.

In just 3 to 4 percent of cases, laser treatment fails to improve the eye condition. For those few restricted cases, a doctor may choose to perform a vitrectomy. After making incisions in the sides of the eye, a small surgical instrument is inserted inside. The instrument chops and gobbles up the blood clots or scar tissue that were clouding the patient's vision. The clouded vitreous is then replaced with a sterile, clear solution that is absorbed by the body as more vitreous is regenerated.

Regardless of the treatment method employed, the important thing to keep in mind is that with early diagnosis and care you can save your eyes.

┃CHAPTER 14

CHILDREN'S EYE PROBLEMS
TREAT THEM EARLY

A little neglect may breed mischief . . .
For want of a nail, the shoe was lost;
For want of a shoe, the horse was lost;
And for the want of a horse, the rider was lost.

Benjamin Franklin, *Poor Richard's Almanac*

To paraphrase Ben Franklin: For want of early treatment, a child's sight was lost.

Your children can naturally outgrow many things with or without your help: sibling rivalry, the need for a night-light, even puppy love. They will not, however, ever recover from amblyopia or strabismus—two serious childhood eye disorders—without help. If these problems are not caught and treated early in childhood, the conditions can last a lifetime—a lifetime of poor vision. On a brighter note, the earlier these problems are diagnosed and the earlier treatment starts, the earlier normal vision can be restored.

These and other eye problems can start early—as early as birth. In fact, one of the first things a doctor does to a baby after it is born—besides spanking it, of course—is put some drops of silver nitrate into its eyes to prevent the possibility of an eye infection from gonorrhea. If the mother were infected, the baby could pick up such an infection during delivery. Some states allow erythromycin ointment to be used as an alternative to silver nitrate. This antibiotic combats both gonorrhea and chlamydia, another common cause of neonatal eye infection.

Unlike puppies, which spend their first few days with their eyes closed, babies see the world as soon as they enter it. But even though they can see at birth, they don't see all that well. Their eyes are still developing, as is their ability to use them.

A baby's visual development actually starts in the womb during the fourth week of pregnancy. At that time, the clusters of cells that will develop into eyes are smaller than the head of a pin and are hidden behind a layer of tissue.

Sometimes people—especially expectant mothers—wonder whether a baby actually sees anything while in the womb. It all depends on how you define sight. There isn't any light in the womb for the baby to use to see by, but as discussed in chapter 10, pressure on the eyeball itself can produce dots, spots, and flashes of color called phosphenes. In fact, the optic nerve translates pressure on the eyeball into all sorts of bizarre patterns.

But a baby doesn't begin to see real objects in real light until it is out of the womb. Of course, it has no idea what it is seeing or what anything means, but both the baby's vision and its understanding of what it is seeing will improve with age—provided there are no problems.

Shortly after birth, all babies should receive an eye screening in the nursery by a pediatrician, family doctor, or—in the case of an infant with a high risk of eye problems—an ophthalmologist. In a typical screening, the doctor looks at the eyes with a penlight, conducts a light reflex test, and checks the retinas with an ophthalmoscope.

High-risk babies, who receive a more careful screening by an ophthalmologist, are those with a family history of retinal problems, cataracts, or other diseases that could affect the eye. Premature children are at especially high risk (see chapter 11). Another high-risk group are those children with a family history of retinoblastoma, a rare eye cancer that is often hereditary (see "An Early Warning of Eye Cancer" on the opposite page).

An Early Warning of Eye Cancer

Retinoblastoma is a rare eye cancer that is often hereditary. It strikes about 500 infants and children in the United States each year.

In the hereditary form, a retinoblastoma gene is passed from parent to child. But the disease can also be nonhereditary, occurring when a new mutation spontaneously occurs in the eyes of a child whose parents did not have the disease.

Fortunately, the hereditary form of the disease can be spotted early through genetic "fingerprinting." If one of the parents had the disease, a blood test is taken and analyzed. The defective gene that caused the cancer can be spotted in the parent's blood and then compared to the genes found in a sample of the baby's blood. If there is a match, the child should be checked frequently for signs of emerging disease.

According to Thaddeus F. Dryja, M.D., associate professor of ophthalmology at Harvard Medical School, the defect in the gene causing the disease "can be as small as one wrong nucleotide, or gene subunit, in a gene that is 200,000 nucleotides long."

If an eye tumor does develop, early treatment with radiation therapy, laser surgery, or cryotherapy may save both the baby's eye and life.

Stages of Visual Development

Regardless of whether your child is a high-risk or normal-risk baby, you can expect certain levels of visual development during the first years of life.

A newborn, for example, usually prefers to look at objects that are close. Newborns also like to look at faces and brightly colored or moving objects.

A one month old's ability to see is much more developed than that of a newborn. And by the time babies are three months old, their vision has developed to the point that they can smoothly follow a moving object, such as a rolling toy, and visually "hold on" to it even when it stops. This is also the time when they really begin to appreciate the colors and moving parts of crib toys such as mobiles. Such toys provide stimulation that may help a baby's vision develop.

Somewhere between the third and sixth month of life, the retina becomes fairly well developed and the baby can actually see small details. The baby can also look from something close to something far away and then back again without getting visually "lost." Depth perception, the ability to judge distances, also starts to develop at this time.

By six months, the eye is about two-thirds of its adult size. Both eyes are usually working together in tandem so the baby has good binocular vision and is developing better distance vision and depth perception. A baby's routine physical at age six months should also include a vision screening to make sure everything is developing normally.

Young children naturally practice eye-hand coordination, and this is well under way by age one. Development of this skill can be enhanced and stimulated by games involving grasping, pointing, tossing, rolling, placing, and catching.

Between the ages of two and five, most children are eager to look at and study pictures, and they even like to draw their own. Picture books and anything else that tells them a story directly connected to what they are seeing helps children coordinate their hearing and vision.

The visual system continues to develop as the child grows, until about nine years of age. At that point, the system is completely developed.

Measles? Dim the Lights

Measles does more than make the skin break out in spots. It can also lead to a corneal infection that makes the eyes sore, teary, and very sensitive to light.

Being in bright light will not damage the eyes, but it will hurt and make the patient a lot more uncomfortable. So when you fluff your measles sufferer's pillows, turn down the lights, too.

That's why a child's first complete eye examination should come before the third birthday. If a child has an eye problem such as strabismus or amblyopia—which we will look at in detail later in this chapter—correcting it could take years. And if it isn't corrected while the child is still relatively young, it might be too late.

Signs That Signal Trouble

Quite often children don't know that there is anything that needs to be corrected because they don't have anything to compare their vision to (see "Discovering the Details" on page 173). How, for example, could a person know that chocolate ice cream tastes better than radish ice cream if they've never had chocolate ice cream?

But it is usually possible to figure out if your child is developing eye problems. Here's some advice from the National Society to Prevent Blindness, which says you should make an appointment with an eye doctor if your child does any of these things.

- Rubs eyes excessively
- Shuts one eye or keeps it covered
- Tilts head or thrusts head forward at an unnatural angle
- Has problems reading or doing other close work, or holds objects close to eyes
- Blinks frequently or is irritable when doing close work
- Is unable to see distant things clearly
- Squints eyelids together or frowns

You should also call the doctor if your child has:

- Crossed eyes
- Red-rimmed, encrusted, or swollen eyes
- Recurring sties of the eyelids

If your child complains of any of the following, a visit to the eye doctor is strongly recommended.

- Eyes itch, burn, or feel scratchy

- Inability to see well
- Dizziness, headaches, or nausea following close work
- Blurred or double vision

While you should always pay attention to any potential vision problems, you should pay special attention if your child is in one of the high-risk categories. These include:

- Children born prematurely
- Children with a family history of eye problems such as childhood cataracts, amblyopia, strabismus, or tumors
- Children whose mothers have health problems such as diabetes
- Children who have had any sort of eye injury, because complications from the injury might not appear until much, much later. Such complications may include glaucoma or cataracts.

Leukokoria's Many Causes

A leukokoria is a white pupil that some infants or children develop. When it occurs, it can indicate any of a number of conditions, some of which are life or sight threatening. Early diagnosis is the key to successful treatment.

The white pupil can be caused by a detached retina, hemorrhaging within the vitreous, or an intraocular inflammation, as well as a number of rare hereditary and developmental problems. Some of the more common and dangerous causes include the following.

Cataracts. This is the most common cause of leukokoria, affecting approximately 1 out of every 250 babies. While some cataracts are mild and pose little danger, others can require surgery within the first few weeks of life if the baby is to ever have a chance of normal vision.

Retinoblastoma. This cancer is the most dangerous cause of leukokoria, and the most common intraocular malignancy of childhood. It can lead to blindness and even death. It occurs in approximately 1 of every 20,000 live births. The prognosis is directly related to how far the cancer has spread throughout the eye—or beyond the eye—and how soon it is diagnosed and treated.

Retinopathy of prematurity (ROP). This disorder is usually associated with premature birth, low birth weight, and oxygen administration. While ROP disappears in 85 percent of all cases, it can also lead to blindness or other vision problems (see chapter 11).

Persistent hyperplastic primary vitreous (PHPV). This is an abnormality in the development of the eye. The affected eye is usually smaller than the other eye. In some instances, prompt surgery must be performed to save the baby's vision.

Discovering the Details

Like millions of other young children, Cathy didn't know she had anything less than perfect vision until her teachers noticed that her work and classroom participation improved when she sat close to the blackboard. They recommended an eye examination, and the doctor prescribed glasses for her.

Her first day with her brand-new glasses, she came running into the house very excited. "Did you know," she told her parents, "there are individual leaves on trees?"

"Lazy" Eye and Amblyopia

Technically, there is no such thing as an eye that is lazy, but the term is used loosely to refer to an eye that is weak. A "lazy" eye could be one that does not see as well as its fellow eye, that cannot be fully corrected with glasses to see 20/20, or that looks off to the side while its partner—the "good" eye—looks straight ahead.

A person with amblyopia has one eye that did not develop normal sight during early childhood. The weak or "lazy" eye is called amblyopic.

Amblyopia is a very common condition, affecting approximately 4 out of every 100 people. It must be treated early, or the baby's vision can be permanently affected.

The most common cause is strabismus—misaligned or crossed eyes—which we will look at next. Other common causes include visual problems that can be corrected with glasses, such as nearsightedness, farsightedness, or astigmatism. Cataracts and other eye diseases can also cause amblyopia, but they are relatively rare in babies.

Because the average baby can't be expected to read the letters on an eye chart—or even name the squares, circles, triangles, ducks, or other shapes on a child's eye chart—it can be difficult to detect a weak eye.

An eye doctor will usually observe how a baby responds and looks at things when first one and then the other eye is covered. If the baby does have an amblyopic eye, he might try to look around or get rid of what is blocking the good eye when it is covered. An eye doctor can also look inside the eye for abnormalities such as cataracts, tumors, inflammations, or other problems.

Patching Takes Patience

If the doctor determines that the affected eye has potentially good vision, the child has to be taught to use the weak eye. This is usually done by patching the stronger eye to build up the weaker eye's strength. In terms of what babies like to do, this is not a popular pastime. If a baby sees a bright and clear picture out of one eye and a dark or blurry picture out of the other, it is only natural to fight having the good eye covered.

Occasionally an eye doctor will use special eyedrops to blur the vision in the good eye or prescribe glasses that improve the vision in the bad eye and worsen the vision in the good one. This, however, is not done very often.

Patching must be done under a doctor's supervision, and the instructions must be carefully followed, because it is possible to weaken the good eye through excessive patching.

The important thing to remember about amblyopia is that it can be corrected, but only if it is diagnosed and treated during infancy or early childhood—by age seven or eight. After that age, the imprint of blurred images is so fixed in the brain that treatment does not seem to help.

It's as if the brain has decided that the amblyopic eye can never recover and refuses to even consider the possibility that it might.

Shiver Me Timbers, 'Tis the Pirate Baby!

Patching is the most basic and helpful method of preventing or correcting amblyopia. And with a little imagination, effort, and investment in arts and crafts supplies, you can even add some fun to this treatment, if the doctor should prescribe it.

Because the stronger eye needs to be covered for weeks at a time, it is understandable that a child will fight having to wear the patch, no matter how persuasive or well intentioned your reasoning and eloquence might be. After all, if millions of adults can gleefully ignore all the medical evidence against smoking or drinking or eating too much, what makes you think a child will care about anything except the immediate need to have a clear view of the world?

That's when the imagination, effort, and arts and crafts supplies come in. *Decorate the patch.*

Turn it into a pirate's eyepatch, or a television screen, or anything that will make your child a little more willing to put up with the inconvenience of wearing it. Maybe everyone in the family can submit "designs" for the patch, and let the child choose from among them. Since the patch has to be changed on a regular basis, there is plenty of room—and need—for a wide variety of designs and any other props that can make patch wearing easier to put up with.

When decorating a patch, remember that the patch must cover the entire eye so that no light can get into it. Adhesive patches work best. Cloth patches, or those attached to the lens of the child's eyeglasses, are too easy to cheat with by looking "around" them or just pulling them off.

The earlier patching starts, the more effective it will be. If patching does not begin before the child reaches the age of six or seven, it may be too late to correct the problem.

Regular eye tests are needed during the patching period to measure the progress of the weaker eye, and also to make sure that the stronger eye does not start to weaken from lack of visual stimulation.

Straightening Out Strabismus

Strabismus is the term used to describe any condition in which the eyes are not straight; people with strabismus may have crossed eyes, walleyes, or one eye that looks up while the other looks down.

While adults can sometimes develop strabismus (see "A Grown-Up Problem" below), it usually occurs in children. In fact, 5 percent of all youngsters are affected.

A Grown-Up Problem

Although most adults with strabismus are people who did not have the problem corrected when they were children, it is possible for an adult to develop the condition.

The most common cause is eye muscle paralysis brought on by diabetes, thyroid disease, stroke, tumors, cataracts, or retinal diseases. Very often this kind of paralysis is only temporary; it gets better with time or with treatment of the underlying disease that caused it. For those who don't get better, prisms can be incorporated into glasses, or surgery may be tried to straighten the eyes.

It is easy to be fooled by "false strabismus" in a baby. An infant's nose is flat and undeveloped, and there may be an extra fold of skin on either side. This fold may cover up the inner white portion of the eye, the sclera, and make the eye appear to be crossed. As the child grows older, the bridge of the nose narrows and the skin is drawn up so that the fold disappears.

People with true strabismus might be bothered by it all the time, or only when they are tired, ill, or looking at an object close to their face. But no matter how or when it affects vision, the underlying cause is that the two eyes are not working together.

Baby's First Home Eye Test

Infants often look as if they have crossed eyes. There is a simple test to find out if that's really the case. Hold a penlight in front of your baby's eyes so that the light reflects back from both of them.

If the reflection is centered in each pupil (the black center of the colored part of the eye), then your baby's eyes are probably straight. If one of the reflections is off-center, make an appointment with an eye doctor.

There are six muscles attached to the outside of each eyeball that move the eye in all directions. Each eye is coordinated with the other through elaborate nerve connections in the brain. This mechanism normally keeps the eyes working together regardless of what they are staring at.

In strabismus, however, the two eyes do not work together. Rather, one eye—the "weak" one—will turn up, down, in, out, or follow slightly "behind" the "strong" one.

Why? We aren't 100 percent sure. But we assume that it is caused by an imbalance in the nerve impulses to the muscles controlling the two eyes.

Making Faces
Can't Make Kids Cross-Eyed

Remember when your mom told you that if you crossed your eyes they'd get stuck in that position and not only would no one ever want to marry you, you would also look funny for the rest of your life?

Mom was wrong. And so was Dad, Grandpa, Aunt Adelaide, and anyone else who told you that if you crossed your eyes too long they would "stick" that way. There has never been a single case on record of a person whose eyes got "stuck" while they were being crossed or because they were being crossed.

Sorry, Mom.

When the two eyes work together properly, they view an object from slightly different positions. The two separate images travel through the optic nerve and are fused together in the brain.

But if the two eyes are looking in two different directions, they are seeing two very different objects at the same time. Instead of fusing the two views together, this can lead to double vision.

The brain hates double vision—absolutely hates it. Why? Because it can't cope with it. So it takes the simple way out and just ignores one of the two images that is being transmitted to it—usually the more blurry of the two. It treats it as if it isn't there and after a while, it isn't.

The brain, in effect, fires the "bad" eye—permanently. And it can't be forced to "rehire" it.

Because of the very real danger that vision will be lost in the weak eye, treatment should begin as early as possible. There are three important goals in treating strabismus.

- To preserve vision
- To make the eyes straight
- To make the eyes work together

Reaching these goals can require years of treatment, often difficult treatment that could require patching, eyeglasses, or even surgery.

Surgery That Balances the Eyes

Although wearing glasses or a patch might be adequate for treating mild strabismus, those tactics may not have much effect on more advanced cases. Many children need surgery on the muscles controlling the afflicted eye.

This is a safe and fairly simple operation in which the tension of the eye muscles is adjusted so that both eyes work together. Either one or both eyes may be operated on. Strabismus, after all, is a problem of balance between the eye muscles, and even though one eye may appear to be straight, both eyes might need adjusting.

The most common type of strabismus operation is done in a hospital and requires that the child be kept overnight. The child is put to sleep for the operation, in which the muscles controlling the two eyes are actually moved.

Why do the muscles have to be moved?

Take a 12-inch ruler and balance it on your finger. The balance point is in the middle, at the 6-inch mark. This can be compared to a well-balanced set of eye muscles. The balance point is in the center.

Now place two quarters on one end of the ruler. The balance is thrown off. The only way to rebalance it is to move your finger away from the middle of the ruler and closer to the two quarters.

A child with strabismus has eye muscles like the unbalanced ruler. Because the eye muscles are of different strengths, a new balance point must be found. If the muscles on the side surfaces of the eyeballs themselves are repositioned, they can exert either greater or lesser pressure to move the eyes in a balanced way.

There is a problem, however. When you tried to find the new balance point on the unbalanced ruler, you probably had to try several times. The same can be true with rebalancing the eyes. A second operation is often required, and sometimes a third. After all, each child's muscular development is unique.

While the operation usually lessens the eyes' degree of turn, glasses and patching might still be necessary. Sometimes eye exercises are also prescribed. Known as orthoptic exercises, these are intended to help the two eyes move together and to encourage the fusing of the two images seen by the eyes. These exercises are especially helpful after surgery for a child whose eyes are now almost straight.

Keep in mind that surgically straightening the eyes doesn't always allow the child to use both eyes more effectively. Sometimes it just makes the eyes appear straight without helping the vision.

A Toxin That Treats

Surgery is not the only method of straightening eyes. Sometimes the doctor uses poison.

A potent nerve toxin, botulinum, can be injected into the stronger of the two eye muscles in minute amounts—usually starting with an injection of just one-billionth (0.000000001) of a gram. The toxin temporarily paralyzes and weakens the muscle, causing it to stretch. By injecting just the right amount, a turned eye can sometimes be made straight. Although not always as permanent as surgery, as many as one-third of strabismus patients are said to be helped by this treatment.

Pulling Strings

Surgeons have developed a procedure to do away with the need for a second—or third—strabismus operation. But it's not for the squeamish.

It's called "the adjustable suture technique," because the surgeon leaves long sutures attached to the eye muscles after the initial surgery. These sutures, or strings, stick out of the eye socket next to the eyeball. When the strings are pulled, the eye muscles will move.

The day after the operation, the surgeon checks the eyes to see if they have been properly adjusted. The patient must be awake and alert for this test. If the eyes are not properly positioned, he pulls the strings attached to the eye muscles until they are, and then ties off the sutures and cuts away the excess string. (The sutures are the kind that will dissolve within the body in a few weeks.)

The procedure is not for everyone. Surgeons normally test their patients' ability to withstand eye irritation before deciding who is a good candidate for it.

The Jumbled World of Dyslexia

Not all medical conditions or diseases act the way you think they should.

The first sign of heart trouble, for example, is often a tingling sensation in the left arm—not in the chest. Sometimes a pain in your hip means that you have a problem in your knee. And an inability to read or understand words because the letters appear to be all mixed up or reversed could mean that a child has a problem inside his brain, not inside his eyes.

Because dyslexia usually manifests as a problem with reading, it has traditionally been associated with the eyes. But although the disorder is not completely understood, current scientific thought treats it as a neurological or perceptual problem. The eyes are sending a clear picture to the brain, but the brain is somehow getting the picture confused.

There are three general classifications of dyslexia.

1. Children with dysphonetic dyslexia cannot read or even sound out words phonetically. To them, words are secret coded messages, and each message has to be learned and memorized separately. A child with this type of dyslexia might "know" the words *dog* and *wood*, but be unable to read the word *dogwood*.

2. Children with dyseidetic dyslexia, which is sometimes called gestalt-blind dyslexia, have trouble memorizing whole words and seeing the differences between similar-looking letters. They can use phonics to interpret the secret code we call writing, but they cannot remember the whole words they struggle to decode. A child with this condition might have to sound out the letters to "read" the word *bicycle* on page one of a story, and then have to struggle all over again when the word reappears on page two. The child might also spell the word as *bysykul*.

3. The third category of dyslexic sufferers are those who suffer from both types, dysphonetic and dyseidetic dyslexia. They are the hardest to help.

Now even though logic would seem to insist that dyslexics must have something wrong with their eyes, no serious scientific studies have ever found any consistent difference between the eyes of dyslexics and nondyslexics. There are no anatomical differences, no chemical differences, no physical differences at all.

Reading specialists, often associated with the schools, help dyslexics "see" more clearly and let them untangle the mysteries of the written word. Different types of visual training have sometimes helped dyslexics overcome their problem. If these approaches work for you or your child, fine. Use them and rejoice.

There is no standard cure or aid that works for all dyslexics, or even for any one identifiable grouping of dyslexics. And when something does work for a specific dyslexic, there may be no scientifically acceptable explanation for why it works.

Look at it this way. Imagine that someone develops a remedy for the common cold. It's given to 1,000 people with colds and all are cured overnight. Voila! A cure! But what if only 1 or 2 or 4 or 5 are cured? Sure, the treatment cures a few people, but it's not a true cure for the condition. It's something that will work on some of the people some of the time.

The same must be said about a "cure" for dyslexia.

There are a wide variety of aids, therapies, and training programs available. And you can't rule them out, because some of them do work in specific cases. But because there is no way to say what will or won't work in any given case—or why—you can't count on them, either.

So if your child has a reading problem, first check to see if it's a vision problem. If it's not, find the experts who can tell you just what type of problem it is. And if it is dyslexia, keep looking until you find the aid or therapy that works. Read up on the subject and learn as much about it as you can.

But whatever you do, don't give up. Your child's future depends on it.

CHAPTER 15

CORNEA SURGERY
RENEWING YOUR EYES

Mathematics, rightly viewed, possesses not only truth, but supreme beauty—a beauty cold and austere, like that of sculpture.

Bertrand Russell, *Mysticism and Logic*

Talking about mathematics in terms of truth, beauty, and sculpture might seem to require quite a mental stretch. But let's take that thought by English philosopher and mathematician Bertrand Russell and stretch those four concepts even further by applying mathematics, truth, beauty, and sculpture to cornea surgery—the cutting, carving, sculpting, and, at times, replacing of our corneas, our windows on the world.

Let's consider the various corneal surgical techniques and procedures in terms of these four concepts.

Mathematics. Every portion or segment of the eye can theoretically be precisely measured, and the measurements can be compared to that of the mythical "perfect" eye.

Beauty. Like any smooth-running and well-designed machine, the eye is a thing of beauty in its own right.

Sculpture. Every eye has its own shape and form. To change the eye itself, you have to change its shape, sculpting a new shape for its surface out of the living material already there.

Truth. There are long and complex philosophical arguments that could be made about the nature and role of surgery. There is also a very short one: Is this operation—and the risk it involves—really necessary?

As discussed in chapter 1, the cornea is the transparent lens that covers the front of the eye. It is one of the body's few living tissues that contains no blood vessels, a fact that bestows two major advantages.

First, it makes the cornea easy to see through. Second, because certain cells in the bloodstream cause the body to reject transplanted organs and tissues, not having any circulation in the cornea increases the odds of a corneal transplant being successful. Please keep all of this in mind as we continue. We'll start out with corneal transplants.

Corneal Transplants— New Eyes for Old

The single most common transplant surgery performed in the world today, corneal transplants have been around for more than 100 years.

Why are corneal transplants so common? Think of the cornea as the crystal covering a watch. It protects the delicate time-keeping mechanism and also allows us to view the face of the watch. But you know how easily your watch crystal can get banged up and scratched. In a similar way, even though the cornea is protected by the eyelids and the blink reflex, it still gets traumatized.

Because of congenital abnormalities, disease, or injury, the cornea may become cloudy or scarred in a way that interferes with normal vision. One of the most common medical reasons for a corneal transplant is eye infection stemming from the herpes simplex virus. For reasons no one really understands, some people are more prone to recurring herpes infections than others. While usually not a major problem, sometimes the infection can lodge deep in the cornea and set up an immune reaction that results in severe inflammation. It can last for months, causing scarring that can make a corneal transplant necessary.

Cornea Swapping's Shaky Start

By the time the first successful human corneal transplant was performed in 1888, people had been talking about the subject—and even doing some experiments—for hundreds of years.

Although serious medical research didn't start until the 1750s, the medical history books mention a charlatan and quack named Chevalier Taylor who roamed Europe in the Middle Ages, making a living by peddling "secret remedies" and potions to the great unwashed, uninformed, and unlettered, which, back then, pretty well summed up more than 99 percent of the population.

Charlatan and quack though he was, Taylor did know what the cornea was, and that if it were scarred or fogged, it could cause blindness. He suggested two ways to solve the problem: Either shave or sand the cornea smooth. He even left precise instructions about how to do it. For shaving, he suggested, "Pare off the excrescence with a small curved knife, leaving as few inequalities as possible." And for sanding: "Scrub the eye with a small brush made of barley bristle."

While history does record his advice, it does not reveal if it was ever followed.

By the mid-1700s, the European medical community was looking at the cornea with a slightly more scientific approach, talking and writing about the possibility of removing cloudy corneas and replacing them with glass, other material, or corneas taken from animals.

Actual transplants—between animals—began in the early 1800s. Then in 1844, a Dr. Kissam in New York transplanted a pig cornea into a human. Later that same year another doctor tried a similar operation using a sheep's cornea. Neither of these "heterografts" (different species transplants) worked.

Those failures did not do much to popularize the experimental operation, especially because all surgery up until that point was done without the benefit of anesthetics.

But in 1846 ether was introduced in Boston, and by 1850 chloroform had been used as an anesthetic in an eye operation. This helped set the scene for an 1859 operation in which glass was implanted in a human cornea.

Finally, almost 30 years later, Dr. Arthur von Hippel, in Germany, was ready to try his hand, ideas, and skill at actually transplanting a human cornea. He had figured out that transplants between members of the same species had a better chance of working. He had also developed a new type of device to remove the old cornea and then cut the replacement cornea so it would fit exactly in its place. In 1888 he performed the first successful human-to-human transplant.

Corneal infections are also becoming more common among contact lens wearers. Most contact lens–related infections are caused by bacteria. A parasitic organism called *Acanthamoeba* has been getting a lot of publicity recently. It causes a serious and hard-to-treat eye infection in a small percentage of contact lens wearers. It is most likely to show up in people who use extended-wear contact lenses or who make their own contact lens saline solution from distilled water they buy in a store. Such distilled water is not sterile and is not meant for use in the eye.

The *Acanthamoeba* has also been found in hot tubs and even in ground soil, so it is very common in our environment. It is believed to cause infections only when a large dose enters the eye and the eye's surface is then irritated by a contact lens or minor injury.

Taking into account everyday trauma, infection, and the fact that many common eye surgery procedures can injure the delicate inner lining of the cornea, it's a wonder doctors don't have to do more corneal transplants.

The number of corneal transplants increases every year. In 1984 there were more than 24,000 performed in the United States. In 1987 there were more than 35,000. And this year? It all depends on the number of available corneas.

A corneal transplant simply replaces the opaque or scarred cornea with a clear one that has been donated in the same way that hearts, kidneys, and other organs are donated after death (see "The Gift That Truly Keeps On Giving" on the opposite page).

The surgery itself is very delicate, and much of it is performed while the surgeon is looking at the cornea through a special operating microscope.

First the opaque cornea is removed with a *trephine*, a round knife that operates a bit like a cookie cutter. The donor cornea is cut to match the hole left by the trephine. Using extremely fine sutures that are thinner than a human hair, the surgeon then sews the new cornea into place.

The operation usually lasts about an hour and is sometimes performed on an outpatient basis. As a rule, the patient is urged to resume a normal lifestyle as soon as possible after the operation (see "Getting Along with Your New Cornea"on page 188). The sutures are usually removed after several months.

The Gift That Truly Keeps On Giving

You can help the blind see. All you have to do is let your corneas be used after you die.

Donated corneas are used for regular transplants, and for research and training. No donated cornea is wasted. As medical knowledge grows and surgical expertise increases, more and more people will be able to see, but only if there are enough corneas available.

Every year people spend months on waiting lists, waiting for a new cornea. And as the number of transplants performed grows, so too does the number of people on the waiting lists. You can help change that by electing to become a cornea donor. In many states there is an organ donor card already attached to each driver's license. In other areas, it's possible to get an organ donor card from a local hospital or eye or organ bank. In any event, talk over your decision with your family. Let them know that you want to help with the gift of sight.

To be useful for either a transplant or research, a cornea must be removed very shortly after death. So to save time and prevent additional emotional strain or trauma, it can help to have a "family policy" about the matter. Every cornea is useful, whether it's a child's or a senior citizen's, and the donor doesn't have to have 20/20 vision.

More than 80 percent of all corneal transplants are successful the first time they are tried. When they do not work the first time, the procedure can be tried again and again. Some patients have received five or six transplants before one "works."

If the transplant is rejected, it will normally happen within the first year following the surgery, and the patient is usually the first one to realize that there are problems. The first indication of rejection can include a slight change in vision, unusual redness, or sensitivity to light. That's what a patient notices. What an ophthalmologist notices is a line of inflammatory cells marching across the inner surface of the cornea like an invading army, leaving destroyed cells in their wake. This can lead to corneal swelling and total transplant rejection.

Getting Along with Your New Cornea

If you are facing corneal transplant surgery, you may hear general statements about what the "average" person will feel like afterward or be able to do, or how long until "normal" vision returns. Just remember that there is no "average" human being. Each and every one of us reacts to things in slightly different ways.

Do not be surprised or necessarily alarmed if your own recovery is different from the so-called, and in many ways mythical, normal one. If you are in doubt or concerned about anything, call your doctor.

When you go home, it is hoped that you will be able to resume living a normal, active life. Here are some considerations to keep in mind. Your doctor will tell you if there are any special circumstances that would change these in your case.

Do . . .

- Resume all *nonstrenuous* activities, including walking and climbing stairs.
- Use both eyes to read or watch TV.
- Use medication as prescribed.
- Use the shower or bathtub, and shampoo if you wish, but try not to get soap or water in the affected eye.
- Wear a metal eye shield or glasses at all times (a patch is optional).

If spotted early, rejection can often be halted with the use of steroid eyedrops.

Researchers are working on ways to reduce the odds of rejection by developing better ways to match donor and recipient tissues. While this can result in a longer wait for a suitable donor cornea to become available, it lessens the chance of a subsequent rejection.

Radial Keratotomy— The Controversial Cuts

According to modern folk legend, "way back" in 1973 a young nearsighted Russian boy got into a fight with another lad who obviously didn't buy into the concept that there is some-

Don't . . .

- Get bumped in the eye
- Swim with your head immersed in water
- Lift anything heavy or participate in strenuous activities, including sports

Expect That . . .

- Your vision will be blurry until the sutures are removed and you are fitted with glasses or contact lenses.
- Your eye may be mildly sore, red, scratchy, and light sensitive for the first few weeks.
- Your stitches will probably not be removed for several weeks or months.

Call Your Doctor If There Is . . .

- A sudden onset of or increase in discharge from the eye
- An increase in or change in the type of eye pain
- An increase in redness of the eye
- A decrease in the clearness of vision in the affected eye

thing intrinsically unfair about hitting a kid wearing glasses. The nearsighted lad wound up with a piece of broken glass stabbing into his eye.

It was a tragedy. At least it started out that way, and it might have stayed a tragedy—a blinding tragedy—except for the fact that the boy's doctor was the noted Russian surgeon, Dr. S. N. Fyodorov.

When Dr. Fyodorov operated on the boy, he removed the broken glass. Then he sewed closed the cuts the glass shards had made in the boy's cornea. But now something was different. The minor changes made in the cornea by the cutting and sewing were enough to alter the shape of the boy's cornea.

Three days later, when the bandages were removed, the boy could see clearly—without his glasses.

Radial keratotomy, often referred to as RK, is the eye operation that Dr. Fyodorov pioneered to correct nearsightedness and allow nearsighted people to throw away their glasses and contact lenses.

There is no doubt that he developed the procedure, although a similar procedure was tried and abandoned 40 years earlier by a Dr. Sato, a Japanese ophthalmologist who cut the cornea on its inner surface.

There is, however, some doubt about when Dr. Fyodorov

"Am I Still Me?"

When they unwrapped the bandages, my once-blind mother looked out at the world and saw it—through a dead man's eyes.

And she cried.

She cried for the man whose eyes she had, for his family, for her own dead eyes, for her years of blindness. She cried with the joy of being able to see again. She also cried with fear. There was a stranger, or at least a part of a stranger, living inside of her.

"Am I still me?"

She'd ask that question from time to time as we sat up half the night discussing the world in general and our lives in particular, and speculating on the nature of the anonymous man who had bequeathed her his vision.

"Am I still me?"

It's a question that more and more of us have to come to grips with every day. There are people walking, working, and running around the world today with mechanical pacemakers marking the beat of their lives by keeping their hearts beating. Millions also pause from time to time to think about the synthetic tubing replacing their arteries, the donated blood flowing through those tubes and arteries, the metal pins in their thighs, the artificial hip joints, their false teeth, their new corneas, even their contact lenses and their wigs.

Where does it stop? Where does the real you stop and the artificial you begin?

Did the "persona" of Terry Fox, the Canadian athlete and can-

developed his procedure. Did he get the idea after seeing the results of his operation on the boy with the cut cornea? Or had he already worked out the procedure in theory before the injured boy presented him with the opportunity to use it? Was there really a nearsighted boy who had his glasses broken in a fight?

The main controversy, however, is not over how or when Dr. Fyodorov developed RK, but over the procedure itself.

---

cer victim who ran across Canada, include the artificial leg he ran on?

"Am I still me?"

To answer that, first answer the following.

"Who am I? What am I? When I say 'me,' just what am I referring to?"

While you're at it, also ask yourself what you are willing to endure to go on being you. When people are considered for transplants, their mental fitness is measured, too. In many cases merely wanting to live is not enough. There must be a driving, consuming passion to survive. That passion must be able to look at a piece of plastic, or steel, or another person's eyes or heart and say: "Mine! Me! That's part of me! That's me! Myself!"

But what, exactly, is self?

A Canadian transplant surgeon, Dr. Calvin Stiller, of London, Ontario, once answered that question this way: "Fundamentally, we are not physical beings, but spiritual. Our physical shell is constantly adapting and being adapted to the environment to protect that spiritual self."

"Am I still me?"

When they unwrapped the bandages, my once-blind mother looked out at the world and saw it—through a dead man's eyes. And she cried.

"Am I still me?"

Yes!

—S.D.

Flattening the Cornea

Compared with most eye surgery, the RK procedure is relatively simple. Four to 16 "radial" cuts are made in the cornea. They look like the spokes on a bicycle wheel. This cutting changes the shape of the eye and, when done right, can correct the eye's focusing power.

As we saw in chapter 3, nearsighted—or myopic—people usually have elongated eyes, so the images their corneas "project" to the retina come into sharp focus before they reach the "screen." By the time they do reach the retina, the images have gone out of focus again.

The RK surgery flattens such corneas so the images they project arrive at the retina in perfect focus. It's like readjusting the lens on a slide projector.

Myopia, or nearsightedness, is the single most common focusing or refractive problem in the world. Most of the people you see wearing glasses are myopic. When you consider how many of these millions of nearsighted people hate having to wear either glasses or contact lenses, it's easy to understand how the RK operation could become popular with patients and lucrative for doctors.

American doctors quickly picked up the RK technique and have performed tens of thousands of the operations. All in all, the results have been surprisingly good. The professional doomsayers who predicted indiscriminate surgery and disastrous complications have, for the most part, been proven wrong.

Most people who undergo the procedure are quite happy with the results, and many recommend the operation to their friends. But even though many patients seem pleased with RK, the medical profession is divided over the ethics of the procedure. Most ophthalmologists are loath to slice into a healthy eye. Nearsightedness, after all, is not a disease. The myopic eye is not sick.

Some doctors opposed to the procedure point out that, historically, eye surgery has been generally reserved for pathological conditions such as cataracts and glaucoma. Doctors taking the other view point out that, historically again, there wasn't much that *could* be done to the eye through surgery except for those pathological conditions. Today, there is; there is RK, cosmetic surgery for the eyes. After all, they add, cosmetic surgery is big business.

Cosmetic surgeons say they help heal a patient's self-esteem by correcting a physical condition that has caused the patient emotional pain. Their attitude is that whether that emotionally disturbing condition be a weak chin, a large nose, or nearsighted eyes, if it can be fixed and the patient desires it, they are willing to fix it.

When Things Go Wrong

The problem is that not all RK procedures turn out the way they were supposed to. Some patients are overcorrected, leaving them farsighted instead nearsighted. Some are not corrected enough, leaving them still nearsighted, sometimes as much as before the surgery. In either case, the patient has had the joy of paying for an operation that did not work, and then having to go out and buy brand-new glasses.

Even when the results are more successful, some patients complain of excessive glare or fluctuating vision, especially during the first few months after the surgery.

One of the problems with the RK technique is that the final result depends on how the patient heals, and no two people heal exactly the same way.

Another point to consider: Because of their nearsightedness, some patients over age 40 are able to read and do other close work without glasses. But when they have RK, they usually lose that ability to read without glasses. They have traded their good reading vision for good distance vision. Of course, they can still read, but now only with glasses.

Alternatives
to Radial Keratotomy

For several years before Dr. Fyodorov introduced RK, Dr. José Barraquer of Bogotá, Colombia, had been reshaping eyes with a group of delicate and precise surgical procedures known as keratophakia and keratomileusis. While Dr. Fyodorov's RK technique is best suited to people with a small or moderate amount of nearsightedness, Dr. Barraquer's procedures work best for people with a high degree of hyperopia (farsightedness) or myopia.

His procedures, however, require both great surgical expertise and computer-controlled equipment. That's part of the reason the techniques have not caught on in North America. They are exceedingly difficult to master.

Another technique, called epikeratophakia, has also gained some attention. And an even newer procedure, called laser corneal sculpting, is also being investigated.

Let's look at each one separately.

Keratophakia

Keratophakia is used to correct a hyperopic, or farsighted, person's vision, usually after cataract surgery. Instead of implanting an intraocular lens (see chapter 8), a donor cornea is obtained from an eye bank and then rapidly frozen. This frozen cornea is then placed on a lathe and precisely cut to form a small lens called a lenticule. The lenticule has to be cut in just such a way that it overcomes the patient's farsightedness.

Once the lenticule has been made, the front half of the patient's own cornea is shaved off with a sharp intrument known as a *microkeratome*. This functions much like a carpenter's plane used to shave or smooth a piece of wood.

The lenticule is then placed over the remaining cornea.

After that, the "shaving" of cornea that was removed from the eye with the microkeratome is replaced over the lenticule and sewn on using extremely fine nylon sutures.

What you have now could be termed a "corneaburger," with the donated and sculpted lenticule in the middle and the two halves of the patient's own cornea serving as the "bun."

If your reaction to this procedure is amazement, read on.

The human cornea is only ½ millimeter thick, about the thickness of a fingernail. It is also curved. The cut splitting it has to be perfect.

The focusing power of the lenticule also has to be perfect if the patient is to see correctly when it's all over.

Several hundred different steps are involved in the operation, and each one of them must also be perfect. Aside from the surgical team, an additional team is required just to make sure that the computerized equipment is working correctly.

Although many surgeons who have studied keratophakia have given up on it in favor of lens implants and other refractive surgical procedures, the results are reportedly good when all the equipment and team members function perfectly. Research is still being done on the procedure, and new developments could make it easier and safer.

A Lenticule with Less Fuss?

As we saw in the chapters on eyeglasses and contact lenses, lenses can be made from a wide variety of substances. That's also true for lenticules—the tiny but vital lens elements employed in keratophakia.

While donor corneas are the usual source, research is being conducted with lenses made of a tongue twister of a compound known as hydroxyethylmethacrylate, the plastic material used for making soft contact lenses. The search is continuing for the best plastic and the most accurate way of cutting it to form suitable artificial lenticules.

Keratomileusis

If you thought keratophakia was tricky, wait until you learn about keratomileusis. While keratophakia can be used only for farsightedness, keratomileusis can be used on both farsighted and nearsighted eyes.

In this procedure, the cornea is once again shaved with a microkeratome. But this time the cornea in question is the patient's own. Instead of sculpting a cornea from the eye bank to serve as a lenticule, the top half of the patient's own cornea is frozen and carved. Once it is carved, it is sewn back on.

There are a number of reasons why keratomileusis is trickier than keratophakia. If the doctor makes a sculpting mistake, the patient has lost half a cornea. While it can be replaced with a donor cornea, the transplant might be rejected. Even if it isn't, it will never be as stable as the patient's own cornea.

Also, in keratophakia, the donated cornea can be frozen and prepared in advance so it is ready as soon as the patient's own cornea has been shaved. But in keratomileusis, the top half of the patient's cornea has to be frozen and carved while the patient is on the table under anesthesia. This just compounds the pressure under which both the surgeon and the rest of the surgical team have to operate.

Epikeratophakia

Epikeratophakia is similar to keratophakia in many respects, but there are a few important differences. Here's what's involved.

First, a donor cornea is obtained. The cornea is frozen and then ground to the right prescription to make a lenticule.

Second, a circular groove is cut into the patient's peripheral cornea, outside the part of the cornea that's looked through. Once the eye has been cut, the surface layer of cells—the epithelium—covering the cut-around area is removed from the cornea.

Third, the lenticule is placed on the denuded surface of the cornea and the edges are tucked into the peripheral groove. The lenticule is then sewn into place with extremely fine nylon sutures.

After several days, the patient's epithelium will grow over and cover the lenticule, helping to hold it in place after the sutures are removed.

This procedure has certain advantages over keratophakia.

- If the lenticule is not the right power, it can be peeled off and the procedure can be repeated.
- Since the incision is made outside the central cornea, there is less chance of scar formation across the visual axis.
- The lenticule does not have to be made by the surgeon during the operation. It can be ordered in a dehydrated state from a supplier who has already ground it to the right prescription—much like a contact lens manufacturer would do.

Epikeratophakia has been used mainly for the correction of farsightedness after cataract operations, especially when there is some risk associated with implanting an intraocular lens. It has also helped infants with congenital cataracts who cannot be fitted with contact lenses. For them, epikeratophakia can be both a sight-saving procedure and an amblyopia preventive (see chapter 14).

Epikeratophakia has also been used for keratoconus, a condition in which the cornea is very distorted. Epikeratophakia helps round out the cornea in some cases.

So far, even though epikeratophakia looks promising, it has not been around long enough for long-term results to be measured. There are a number of areas in which complications could develop.

One possible concern is the fact that the corneal "sandwich" produced by the procedure is rather thick. We don't yet know what the long-term effects of this will be on the endothelium, the inner layer of the cornea that maintains the cornea's clarity.

It is also difficult to make a perfect groove in the surface of peripheral cornea with the instruments that are currently available. These instruments will have to be refined and improved so that ophthalmologists can perform this operation with greater accuracy.

Laser Corneal Sculpting

Unlike keratophakia or keratomileusis, which require temporarily removing or replacing at least part of the cornea, in laser corneal sculpting your cornea never leaves your eye.

Instead, a computer-controlled laser sculpts or reshapes your cornea. And instead of requiring hours on the operating table and days in the hospital, once all the mapping and measuring is done, the actual procedure takes about 10 seconds in your doctor's office.

The key to the procedure is the laser and the computer that operates it. The eye is first mapped and the surgeon determines exactly what parts should be treated. These data are fed to the computer, which prepares the different "shots" the laser will fire. Each nearly overlapping rapid-fire shot is aimed in advance to neatly clip off a different piece of corneal tissue.

You then sit facing the machine and are "centered" on the laser. It starts, and for the 10 seconds it takes, it sounds like a machine gun going off.

If you flinch, cough, blink, sneeze, or make any other move

while the procedure is in progress, the laser will automatically shut off. Because the entire procedure is being videotaped, the video image of what the eye looked like just before the laser was interrupted is frozen and saved. That way the laser can pick up exactly where it left off once you have been repositioned in front of the machine.

Corneal sculpting is designed to work for both nearsighted and farsighted people, people with astigmatism, and those who have had their cataracts removed but have not had an intraocular lens implanted.

Proponents say it could replace many of the other surgical techniques. One way or another, it seems that Dr. Fyodorov's prediction that "someday we will build monuments with our useless eyeglasses" may be destined to come true.

A Costly, Risky Decision

While the nonsurgical procedures that can be used to improve a person's vision are basically limited to glasses and contact lenses, the number of surgical approaches and techniques seems to increase every year.

The entire field of refractive surgery is a new and still somewhat controversial area of ophthalmology. Unlike corneal transplants and other eye operations performed soley for medical reasons, many of these new procedures raise an entirely different issue: What constitutes necessary—and unnecessary—surgery?

Because procedures like radial keratotomy, keratophakia, keratomileusis, epikeratophakia, and laser corneal sculpting are so expensive, the question of affordability is extremely important. While insurance companies may pay for some of these procedures in some situations, they won't in others. That can put sharper vision out of the price range of many people.

People who are considering having one of these operations should literally go out and do their own research, talking to a number of different doctors about benefits, risks, and costs, and carefully making up their own mind before risking their eyes.

CHAPTER 16

HIGH-TECH MEETS LOW VISION
SEEING THE FUTURE

We have the technology. We can rebuild him.

From the opening of "The Six Million Dollar Man" TV show

Researchers are always looking for answers. That's their job. But with the vast and fast progress being made in all areas of medical research, today's researchers are looking for answers to questions that didn't even exist 20, 10, or even 1 or 2 years ago. Questions like:

- How can we perform an eye transplant?
- How can we make an artificial eye that a patient can see with?
- How can the optic nerve be repaired?
- How can we grow a new retina?
- How can we enable the blind to see?

These and other questions, questions that haven't yet even been thought of, will be answered—eventually. Just when and how the breakthroughs come that will lead to these answers will depend on study, research, and experimentation.

Even though we don't know how or when, or even in what order these questions will be answered, we can make at least a few predictions. While some are based on expected progress in science and technology, others are based on already-evident trends in society.

Many of the changes we will have to deal with are being spawned by competition for patients and the health-care dollar. Others are forced on both doctor and patient by a government that is attempting to regulate the medical profession more, while spending less money on federal and state health-care programs.

It is clear that there are a lot more doctors in practice than there used to be. In most medical specialties, the system seems to be oversupplied, and ophthalmology is no exception.

In addition, optometrists, whose numbers are double those of ophthalmologists, are assuming an ever-expanding role in the diagnosis and treatment of eye disease. Many states now have optometric drug laws that allow optometrists to use drugs for the diagnosis and treatment of eye conditions. Whether the scope of optometry will extend to minor surgical procedures and the use of lasers is still unclear.

Some of this competition has been a good thing. Doctors try harder to please their patients and keep them coming back for regular checkups or treatment. As in other markets, the suppliers who satisfy the consumer—and do so at the right price—are most likely to stay in business and be successful.

On the other hand, consumers are often finding that they have fewer choices than they used to. Companies are signing contracts with clinics and health plans to provide medical care for their employees at reasonable rates. Once the contracts are signed, the patients don't always get the doctors they want at the time and place that is most convenient.

High-volume medicine works well under certain circumstances, but there are times when all of us need a little extra attention. Will we get it in the medical marketplace of the future? It's too soon to tell.

New Surgical Horizons

We do know that surgical procedures are getting better, faster, and more successful. Cataract surgery is a good example. Fifteen years ago, patients were kept in the hospital for three days so the doctor could be sure the healing process was taking place on schedule. Now patients go home an hour after their surgery and have very few restrictions on their activities. That's the kind of development that's good for the doctor, the patient, and the health-care system.

Why are today's cataract operations so much better and the recovery so much faster? You can credit better microscopes, better sutures, and better and sharper surgical instruments. And you can bet that things are going to get better still.

As we saw in chapter 8, intraocular lenses have helped people with cataracts get their normal vision back. Contact lenses and intraocular lenses, which replace the traditional post-surgery "Coke bottle" glasses, are constantly being improved.

Bifocal intraocular lenses are also in development. They will let you see both near and far—the theater marquee across the street and the phone book in your hand—without the aid of glasses.

Also likely to become popular: New foldable intraocular lenses that can be rolled up like a taco and slipped into the eye through a tiny incision. Because that incision heals more quickly than a standard incision, visual recovery after cataract surgery will be even faster. We may even have drugs that speed along the healing process and prevent the occasional complication that now occurs.

There may even be drugs one day that prevent cataracts altogether.

You can also be sure that lasers will become an even more important tool for the eye doctor. These focused beams of light are already being used for cutting, burning, and removing diseased parts of the eye (see "This Little Light of Mine, I'm Going to Let It Shine" on page 202).

And as we saw in chapter 15, new advances and developments are constantly being made in reshaping the cornea with lasers and supersharp diamond knives. The aim of this type of high-tech surgery is to correct nearsightedness and other refractive errors.

There is still a great deal of research to be done in this field, because we still don't always know how the eye is going to respond to being reshaped. Not every patient gets the same amount of correction from the same amount of cutting.

In a few years, we may be better able to predict how an individual will respond to a laser cut. Then more people may be able to trade in their glasses for a reshaped cornea.

This Little Light of Mine, I'm Going to Let It Shine

Most diseases are looking for cures. But a laser is a cure looking for more diseases. It is probably the single most important advance in the history of eye treatment in the last 25 years.

Lasers were first used for eye surgery in the 1960s, and since then they have been used to maintain, improve, and in some cases restore sight to countless hundreds of thousands of men, women, and children around the world.

The word *laser* is an acronym. It was created by taking the first letters of five words—*light amplification* by *stimulated emission* of *radiation*.

To create a laser, you put specific gasses in a tube and then pass a powerful electrical current through it. Ophthalmic lasers usually use one of three different gases: argon, which produces green or blue-green light; krypton, which produces a red or yellow light; or neodymium-yttrium-aluminum-garnet (Nd-YAG), which produces an infrared light.

Argon and krypton lasers are referred to as photocoagulators. The light they emit is absorbed by the pigmented tissues in the eye and converted into heat. This heat burns or cauterizes the tissue, leaving scar tissue. This sort of laser is often used to reattach a detached retina or repair retinal tears or holes, because the scars can be placed to hold the retina to the back of the eye. Even though the eye is blind at the spots where it is scarred by the laser, the scars are small and don't interfere with vision.

These lasers are also used in cases of diabetic retinopathy to burn out and close leaking blood vessels in the eye and to try to limit the damage done by macular degeneration. They are also used in cases of sickle-cell retinopathy, a disease most common among black patients.

Lasers are already crucial to treating diseases of the retina, and they will certainly become even more important in the future. As technology improves, so will our ability to better focus the laser beam to wipe out abnormal blood vessels without damaging nearby normal tissue. Our ability to treat macular degeneration and diabetic retinopathy will also improve.

Paralleling these developments in lasers, the pharmaceutical industry is making exciting progress in research programs to develop new drugs to treat diabetes, cataracts, and other prob-

Glaucoma sufferers can also benefit from the argon and krypton lasers, which are used to increase drainage, allowing the release of the blinding pressure caused when fluids build up inside the eye. An argon laser can also be used to remove tumors on the eyelid without damaging the eyelid or even leaving much of a scar.

The Nd-YAG laser is a photodisrupter. Instead of burning the tissue, it destroys it by exploding it. It has many uses, such as the cutting away of iris adhesions and the destruction of vitreous strands that could cause a retinal detachment.

This type of laser is also used after some cataract operations when a patient's membrane begins to cloud up and obscure vision. The laser is used to open a hole in the clouded membrane.

Lasers do all this and more, and they do so without the need of a scalpel, incision, or stitches. This means there's no chance of an infection. The laser also has the ability to pass through the clear portions of the eye without damaging them, or even causing any pain. This means that the procedures can be performed on an outpatient basis.

Thanks to sophisticated microscopic aiming and delivery systems—some of which are actually computer controlled—an eye surgeon can operate at a level of precision impossible with a conventional scalpel.

While the list of uses for lasers in eye surgery is long today, it will be even longer tomorrow as researchers develop both new uses and new lasers. One laser probe being developed could actually be inserted inside the eye itself though a tiny hole—about the size of the hole left by a hypodermic needle—in the sclera. Such a laser would allow a surgeon to operate with even greater accuracy than is possible today.

lems. Such drugs will accurately target certain abnormalities in the body's chemistry, and strike only at them—ignoring everything else.

Our ability to home in on these abnormalities has been greatly enhanced by the sciences of immunology and molecular biology. The high-tech companies you read about in the paper are the innovative pioneers in this futuristic approach to controlling diseases of the eye and other parts of the body.

Finally, we are learning a great deal more about how diseases are inherited and the genetic tendencies that lead to specific medical problems.

As scientists "map" the genetic material, a project that will be completed early in the twenty-first century, we will have a better idea of which tiny part of a chromosome is responsible for which particular characteristic. This will allow us to predict who will develop diabetes, who will lose sight from macular degeneration, and who will get cataracts at an early age. Scientists may also be in a position to prevent a trait from developing (with diet or drugs), or even to modify the genetic material by deleting or replacing the abnormal gene.

It has been said that the next decade will be the biotechnology decade. There is every reason to believe that this is true. Ophthalmology and medical science will certainly be swept along by the new and exciting developments that thousands of brilliant scientists around the world are working on every day.

The ultimate beneficiaries will be the patients who may one day escape the ravages of today's common diseases, and the doctors who strive daily to help their patients.

Low Vision: A Nagging Problem

Despite all of today's high technology and everything else that can be done for the eyes, there are times when nothing works—not surgery, not medication, not taking care of yourself, not even taking all the right vitamins and eating all the right foods and avoiding all the wrong ones.

Low vision still happens—frequently. Next to arthritis and

heart disease, it is the single most common disability among senior citizens. Nearly two million Americans have low vision.

A person has low vision when the vision in his best eye—even while wearing corrective lenses—is somewhat worse than 20/70. Low vision is not blindness. As a rule, a person with low vision can tell that something is there, in front of him, but not what—or even who—it is.

There are numerous causes of low vision: cataracts, glaucoma, macular degeneration, diabetic retinopathy, accidents, birth defects, and the natural aging process are just the most common ones.

There are also numerous types of low-vision problems. Sometimes there are problems with the entire eye. In other cases, such as macular degeneration, a person loses central vision but still has peripheral vision. Other types of low vision include the reduction or loss of color vision, reduced focusing power, and problems adapting to changing lighting conditions.

People with low vision can learn how to use low-vision aids. They will not have 20/20 vision, but they will be able to make good use of whatever vision they have left to read, get around, and lead a fairly normal, active, and independent life.

Although people *can* learn to use low-vision aids, not all of them do. Some refuse to try. Some try for a little while, get frustrated, give up, declare themselves to be blind, and quit trying.

Trying the various low-vision aids, finding the ones that are right for you, and learning how to use them effectively aren't easy. Each step can be hard and frustrating work—but not nearly as hard and frustrating as blindness.

Some people do learn to use the aids but refuse to use them in public. They're embarrassed. As a result, they either turn into hermits, so that no one can see that they have a problem, or they stumble around in public denying that they have any sort of problem.

The keys to learning how to use low-vision aids are motivation, adaptability, realistic expectations, and a willingness to experiment.

There are a variety of low-vision aids, ranging from large-print books and magazines and high-intensity lamps to different types of lenses and electronic image enlargers.

Some are designed for close work and others for distance

vision. Most people need a combination of low-vision aids to use at different times for different vision needs.

More and more eye doctors are beginning to specialize in low-vision training. If you have low vision, and your doctor doesn't handle the condition, ask for a referral to a doctor who does, or to a nonphysician low-vision specialist.

The cost of low-vision therapy and equipment can vary depending on your vision, insurance, age, and current state and federal regulations. In some cases, it could be reimbursable or tax deductible.

Low-Vision Lenses

There is a wide variety of lenses available. These include powerful regular and bifocal eyeglass lenses; hand-held, mounted, or wearable magnifying lenses; and telescopic lenses that mount on a section of your eyeglasses. Research is also under way into the possibility of implanting special lenses directly inside the eyes of low-vision patients.

There are some trade-offs in finding the right lenses. You will probably need several of them for different uses. It is also important to keep in mind that the lower the amount of magnification you use, the wider your field of vision.

There are also inexpensive, flat, plastic magnifying lenses available that can be placed on the page you are reading and can also be used as a bookmark when you are done reading.

People with low vision might also want to keep a pair of binoculars handy, especially when they are outdoors. They are quite handy for viewing street signs, billboards, theater marquees, store signs, and other distant objects.

Low-Vision Electronics

Closed-circuit TV systems are available that let you aim a camera or scanner at what you want to read or see. The image is then enlarged and shown on a TV set or computer screen in front of you.

Many electronic systems can be operated with what is called a joystick, so that the person using it doesn't even have to read and punch a keyboard to control the image being transmitted.

Electronic systems can usually provide greater magnification than optical systems. Many of them are quite portable and are battery powered. In fact, research is already under way to develop a portable electronic low-vision enhancer that could be worn on a person's belt.

Such a system would be like a miniature TV studio that could take pictures of what the patient was facing, process and enhance the images, and then transmit them through optical fibers to special TV-monitor glasses worn by the patient.

Low-Vision Lighting

Proper lighting is often as important as the low-vision aid it is used with. In fact, a good low-vision aid without proper lighting can be useless, whereas a lot of light can help a person see better even without low-vision aids.

As a rule, people with low vision see better under standard light bulbs than they do under fluorescent light tubes. But there are a number of different types of light bulbs. You should experiment with different ones until you find the type you need to see your best.

Large-Print and Talking Books

Both *Reader's Digest* and *The New York Times* publish large-print editions, the same size type that you are reading now, and both are available by mail. Other publications also have large-print editions. There are also large-print reference books such as dictionaries and atlases, as well as large-print crossword puzzle books. Almost all libraries stock large-print books.

Talking books are also available at bookstores or through your local library and the Library of Congress.

Talking books and other material for the blind and the visually impaired can often be mailed postage free. Talk to your local postmaster to find out about the current rules and procedures.

There are also computer programs available that use a scanner coupled with a voice synthesizer to "read" a book or magazine to you.

In some cities there are radio reading services for the visually impaired and handicapped. These radio stations usually broadcast on one specific frequency, and a special radio receiver is required to hear them. The services usually read the local newspapers as well as some national newspapers and magazines, best-selling books, and community news and events.

For information about what kind of help is available in your area, and who to talk to about it, first check with your eye doctor. But don't be surprised if your eye doctor doesn't know. Doctors deal with medicine, not low-vision aids. You can also check with your local department of social services, nearest office of the National Society to Prevent Blindness, or any other local group that deals with the visually handicapped.

Appliances, Gadgets, and Other Aids

There are many aids and appliances for people with low vision. These include:

- Timekeeping devices such as talking digital clocks and other clocks and watches with large numbers, or large numbers that are projected onto a ceiling or wall
- Kitchen appliances such as kitchen timers with extra-large numbers, appliances with large buttons and dials, easy-to-read measuring cups and spoons, and largemouth funnels
- Household gadgets such as large-number push-button phones, large-print playing cards, talking bathroom scales, talking calculators, TV screen enlargers, sewing machine magnifiers, needle threaders, large-print plastic labelers, padlocks that are opened with special magnets, and signature and letter-writing guides that fit over stationery, envelopes, and checks

These and other aids are available from medical and convalescent supply houses and some mail-order catalogs.

You can often devise your own low-vision aids, as well. First determine what it is you have to accomplish and what could be done to make it easier. Here are ten examples.

- Replace fluorescent fixtures with conventional lights.
- Exchange talking letters with friends and family. Send cassettes back and forth.
- Put a bright light in your closet so you can see exactly what clothes you are taking out and whether they match.
- Replace your telephone notepad and pencil with a large pad of paper and a fat felt-tip pen to make sure that all notes are written large and dark enough to be read.
- Buy large, brightly colored, and distinctively shaped containers for food, drinks, pills, or other things you use every day.
- Get a large key ring, something that you cannot over-look.
- You can also buy little plastic circles that fit on the round ends of your keys. They come in different colors and textures so you can find a specific key more easily.
- Make sure all medication is labeled in large print.
- If you have to take liquid medicine, you can get a tube-type measuring spoon at almost any pharmacy. Use a dark felt-tip pen to mark off the measuring point to show how much you have to take.
- Spend some time learning to tell the difference between coins by feel. Pennies, nickels, dimes, and quarters are all different sizes and weights, and with a little practice you should be able to tell the difference without looking at them. Separate your paper money in your wallet by denomination. Keep $1 bills in one section of your wallet. Keep your $5 bills next to them, but folded in half. Stick $10 and $20 bills in other parts of your wallet.

With a little forethought and some help from technology both simple and advanced, you can learn to make the most of your vision—even low vision.

CHAPTER 17

A LIFETIME OF SIGHT
HEALTHY EYES
FOR WORK AND PLAY

One of the most common questions an eye doctor hears: "Doctor, can I wear out my eyes if I read too much?"

Answer: "No!"

If General Motors, Ford, and Chrysler could make cars the way God makes eyes, you would never see a foreign-made auto on American highways. For no matter how much you use your eyes to read, watch TV, or do crossword puzzles, you cannot wear them out.

Legend has it that Galileo's vision deteriorated after years of looking through the telescope he invented. It was purely coincidental. His vision deteriorated as he got older. It happens to many people whether or not they spend hours looking through a telescope. Saying that you can wear out your eyes by seeing through them is like saying that you can wear out a window by looking out it.

If, for example, corneas were not meant to last as long as

the body they were issued to—and quite often longer—they would not be able to be reused for transplant surgery after the original owner's death. Of course, even the most carefully made piece of machinery can break down if it is abused. And while there are many ways to abuse and damage your eyes, reading is not one of them.

Up Close and Personal: Tired Eyes

But what about eye fatigue or eyestrain, we hear you ask. Doesn't that prove that too much reading will wear out my eyes?

No. Even though eyestrain is usually associated with reading or doing other close work, it does not damage the eye. It just tires the eye.

To be more accurate, it's not the eye itself that gets tired or strained, but the muscles around the eye. Move your eyes back and forth or up and down repeatedly for a long period of time and the muscles controlling them react the same way that the ones controlling your feet do after running a marathon. They ache.

When you focus on something very close, you are flexing the muscles that adjust the lens inside your eye. That also requires muscular work.

The amount of work—muscular tension—increases as the quality of the working conditions decreases. It is easier to read in a well-lit room than in a dim one, for example, and easier to read while sitting or standing still than while driving over a bumpy road. It's also easier to read when you are rested than when you are tired. And if you need reading glasses, it is easier to read while wearing them than it is to try to read without them.

These may sound like self-evident rules, but you'd be amazed at the number of people who need glasses but refuse to wear them while they read in dimly lit rooms—and then complain about how bad their eyes are and how terrible the suffering is that they have to go through.

It's a lot like the old joke: This guy goes to see his doctor, and while he's talking to him he lifts his right arm as high as it will go, and then twists it behind his own back until he can grab the back of his pants. By the time he has hold of his pants he is literally doubled over in pain.

"Doctor," he says, "Every time I do this it hurts."

"Very interesting," says the doctor, studying the strange and obviously painful shape his patient had contorted himself into. "Have you ever considered not doing it?"

The same applies to eyestrain. It can be avoided. But if you forget to avoid it, it will disappear anyway.

How to Ease the Strain

As a rule, you do the same things to treat eyestrain as you do to avoid it—you remove the cause. Here are some ways to do just that.

If you are in bright sunlight, wear sunglasses. If you don't have any, at least wear a hat with a wide enough brim to shade your eyes. If you have both, wear both.

Avoid reading for any length of time in a car or other moving vehicle, especially if the movement is rough or jerky. You should also avoid reading while lying flat on your back or propped up on an elbow. If you like to read in bed, use a pillow or two so you can read sitting up.

Make sure you have adequate light for whatever it is you are doing—sewing, reading, or doing any other close work.

Don't get too far away or too close to the work you are doing. If you're reading, the book or paper should generally be between 16 and 21 inches away from your eyes—depending on what you personally find comfortable—and a little bit below eye level. It's easier to read while looking down than while looking up.

If you already have eyestrain and are looking for relief, stop using your eyes. Put your head back and your feet up and close your eyes for a few moments. Dim the lights. Put a damp washcloth over your eyes. Relax. And don't worry about it.

When the muscles in your legs ache, it doesn't mean that

you have damaged your legs. It means that you have used them and they need a rest. Once they've rested, they'll be ready to go again. It's the same with your eyes.

The Proper Way to Watch TV

Television is another area of concern. While it's often said half-jokingly that watching too much TV may permanently damage the brain, there is no scientific evidence that it will do the same to your eyes—or even to your children's eyes. But as with reading, sewing, and other close work, you can develop eyestrain if you don't watch TV properly. What is the best way to watch TV? First make sure that you have a clear and sharp picture that isn't vibrating or jumping around. And while a TV set might make a great night-light in an otherwise dark room, if you're actually going to be watching it you may be more comfortable if other lights in the room are on. Soft, indirect lighting is best. Just make sure that it doesn't reflect off the screen into your eyes. Glare is one of the most common causes of eyestrain.

How far you sit from the screen is a matter of personal taste and comfort, as is the size of the screen. But be aware of your own vision needs. Remember, the closer you sit the harder your eye muscles will have to work to focus on the screen. Another concern about sitting too close is seeing too much: All the distortions and interference become more obvious and aggravating.

You don't have to have your eyes glued to the set. It's like keeping your muscles flexed all the time. Eventually they get tired, and they let you know they are tired by aching. So let your eyes wander from time to time. Who knows? You might even find something or someone more interesting to look at.

You should also place the TV so the screen is at eye level and straight in front of you. Looking at a TV screen from off to one side just makes the picture appear distorted, and that speeds up eyestrain.

Now, if you do all of this and still get frequent "television headaches," the problem may not be eyestrain but something more serious. See your doctor. And by the way, the TV set didn't cause the problem.

Can Color TV Zap Your Eyes?

Back when color TVs were first starting to become popular, there was a great deal of public concern about the x-rays they emitted. Those concerns were valid, because the Bureau of Radiological Health eventually announced controls and standards for TV picture tubes.

No TV set was allowed to emit more than 0.5 milliroentgen per hour, even under the most adverse operating conditions. Every set manufactured since January 15, 1970, has had to carry a label certifying its compliance with that standard. To ensure compliance, the bureau randomly spot-checks TV sets from various manufacturers on a regular basis. In addition, TV repair people can use x-ray detectors to determine if sets are emitting too much radiation.

Although the labeling was not required until 1970, the vast majority of TV sets were meeting those requirements by the end of 1968. If you have an old color TV set manufactured before then, you can have a TV repair shop check it out.

Although stringent limits were set, color TV x-ray radiation was never considered a serious problem. The dosages were small. But the long-term effects of low-level radiation can be harmful.

By the way, black-and-white TV sets do not produce x-rays strong enough to make it out of the picture tube.

Computers:
A Special Problem?

Half of all computer users complain of tired eyes, blurred vision, light sensitivity, tearing, and red eyes.

What is responsible? Do these conditions present any real hazards? Could even more serious problems develop later, after years and years of computer use?

So far, there is no evidence that video display terminals (VDTs) cause any kind of eye damage. The American Academy of Ophthalmology and the National Research Council consider VDTs to be safe for normal use. There is no evidence that they cause cataracts or damage the eyes in any other way. We also know that they do not emit any hazardous amounts of radiation.

There is no doubt, however, that VDTs do produce eyestrain. After all, you are concentrating on the screen for long hours. Now while it's true that people also spend long hours concentrating on books, as a rule, books do not:

- Reflect light or glare directly into the eyes
- Emit their own light
- Flicker and shimmy

This is why eye complaints are among the most important concerns of both occupational health experts and the entire computer industry.

As you learned earlier in this chapter, there is a big difference between straining the eyes and actually damaging them. But straining the eye muscles in front of a VDT can be as serious a medical problem as straining any other muscles, especially because they are the muscles you need to use every day at work.

Spending long hours at a VDT—whether for programming, word processing, running a spread sheet, or playing computer games—translates into hours of intense reading and concentration in front of an illuminated, flickering screen. The eyes get quite a workout tracking the words, symbols, numbers, or other figures, and from jumping back and forth between different parts of the video display. Temporary discomfort and vision problems are frequently the result.

But the screen is not the only culprit. Quite often the rest of the office is as much to blame as the computer.

Many offices were not designed with VDTs in mind. The desks are not the right height to allow for comfortable viewing of the screen or operation of the keyboard. The style of the chair makes it awkward to get close enough to the desk, the screen, or the keyboard.

The way the furniture and equipment are arranged, the location of the electrical outlets, the type of lighting being used—

all of these can make using a computer a physically draining and demanding experience.

If the physiological problems don't get you, maybe the psychological ones will. Many workers cannot adjust to the technological revolution and the new innovations of the modern working environment. They are used to doing the same things the same way they have always done them. They don't like change. Some will fight it—sometimes overtly and sometimes covertly. Sometimes they won't even realize that they are fighting it.

Some workers also have an underlying fear of being replaced by a computer. Many of those fears may be well founded.

But regardless of the type of concern they have, and whether or not it is justified, such worry causes stress. And stress can be focused, or manifest itself, in particular parts of the body—often in the eyes.

Changing the color of computer screens or making them more "friendly" in other ways will not have much effect on people who are opposed to change in general, and technological change in particular. If people are afraid that they will be replaced by a computer, the model, style, and features of the computer that replaces them are moot points. For some people, the only solution to "computer-induced eyestrain" is a session with a psychologist.

But a great deal of actual computer-associated eyestrain can be corrected and alleviated by changing the computer, the office itself, or even the desk or chair you use.

Getting Comfortable with Your VDT

The desk or table should be large enough to hold the computer and any other equipment, paperwork, or supplies you need to keep handy. Keyboards should be set at a comfortable height—usually below normal desktop level. The chair should feel comfortable, provide good back support, and make it easy to reach the keyboard.

The screen itself should be between 16 and 21 inches away from your eyes—depending on what is comfortable for you personally. If a computer station is going to be used by a number of different people, eash person who uses it should be able to make adjustments so that the screen is a comfortable distance away.

If there is any sort of clip or board to hold material that is to be typed, it should be placed next to the screen. That way you don't have to constantly change your focus or move your head too much as you read and type.

Room lighting is a major consideration, too, or at least it should be. Many find fluorescent lights both harsh and annoying. Soft lights that minimize shadows and glare but adequately illuminate reading matter are probably the best for preventing tired eyes. Glare of any kind will quickly produce fatigue and discomfort in many individuals.

Indoor glare may result from the use of unshielded light bulbs or improperly placed light sources. This can be avoided by the use of indirect lighting. Avoid having a single strong source of light in an otherwise dark room. Bright light against a dark background can very quickly lead to eye fatigue.

The final word on VDTs is not in yet. We still do not have a good standardized method to measure eye fatigue. But we do know that many VDT users suffer eye discomfort and visual fatigue beyond what is expected in a normal workplace.

Why? We don't know—yet. And we won't know until more research has been done.

Good Nutrition
Is Important

There is no doubt that good nutrition is necessary for good vision. After all, malnutrition is one of the leading causes of blindness in Third World countries.

There is also no doubt that, in some instances at least, certain vitamins can help prevent or delay the development of certain conditions. But which vitamins will help which conditions?

As already noted elsewhere in this book, vitamin A is absolutely essential for good vision. It is a key ingredient in the chemical reaction that lets the retina convert light into the electrical impulses that our brains interpret as sight. But the same light that enters our eyes with images can also damage our eyes. And there again, vitamin A may be able to help.

When light hits the molecules in our eyes, it breaks off small, highly charged particles of oxygen called free radicals. There is some evidence that these free radicals can damage tissue when they run into it. There is also speculation that one of the tissues most prone to this sort of damage is the macula—the central portion of the retina that is responsible for most of our direct vision.

Why Rabbits Don't Wear Glasses

Vitamin A is a key ingredient in the chemical reaction that lets the retinas of our eyes convert light into the electrical impulses that our brain interprets.

A major source of this vitamin is fish-liver oil. Another important source of vitamin A is a substance called carotene, which is found in carrots and other orange-colored fruits and vegetables.

Vitamin A is the reason that Mother was right: Carrots are good for your eyes.

Macular degeneration is a leading cause of vision loss for the elderly. But there is some preliminary evidence that people who eat more fruits and vegetables rich in vitamin A are less likely to develop macular degeneration. Vitamin A is one of the substances—scientists call them antioxidents—that absorb oxygen free radicals, soaking them up like a sponge. Good sources of vitamin A include carrots, squash, pumpkin, apricots, and Brussels sprouts.

In areas of the world where vitamin A is almost totally lacking from the diet, severe night blindness, dry eye conditions, and tear deficiencies often develop. But in the United States, Canada, and most of the rest of the developed world, such severe vitamin A deficiency is practically unknown.

Research is also being done with a vitamin A ointment, which some researchers think helps speed up healing after eye surgery. And as we saw in chapter 11, a very small number of people suffering from retinitis pigmentosa (RP) can be helped by taking extra vitamin A. Similar results have been found with vitamin E. The vitamins have slowed down and even stopped the spread of RP in some cases. In others, they have had no effect at all. Or they could even make the condition worse. So talk to your doctor before trying this form of treatment.

Vitamin E, which is especially abundant in vegetable oils, might also have some value in combating retinopathy of prematurity, a condition that blinds premature babies. Tests have shown that it does interfere with the proliferation of blood vessels in the eyes of kittens with retinopathy. Will it work in humans? No one knows for sure, yet.

How does vitamin E work for kittens? The best guess is that it acts as an antioxidant, scavenging oxygen free radicals.

The B vitamins—including thiamine (B_1), riboflavin (B_2), niacin, pantothenate, pyridoxine (B_6), folate, and B_{12}—are also necessary for vision. Doing without them completely could lead to optic nerve damage and total blindness. The B vitamins are found in meats, milk, vegetables, and whole-grain breads.

Vitamin C, or ascorbic acid, is found in many fruits and vegetables—especially in oranges, lemons, and tomatoes. Other research has indicated that taking 300 to 600 milligrams of vitamin C or 400 international units of vitamin E daily for a number of years may reduce the chances of cataracts developing with age. But as with so many nutritional studies, there is an indication that it might work, but no conclusive proof.

Zinc is another nutrient that could prove beneficial to your eyes. As with vitamin A, a deficiency has been linked to night blindness in some studies. And as we saw in chapter 12, there is one study that suggests that taking oral zinc supplements may retard vision loss in some cases of macular degeneration.

But while we need to be aware of foods and nutrients that are good for us, we also have to be aware of what isn't. Citrus fruits, for example, which are loaded with necessary vitamin C, can occasionally make eyes more sensitive to ultraviolet radiation. Celery also contains chemicals that do the same thing, as do birth control pills, antibiotics, blood pressure medications, antihistamines, and some cosmetics. So if your eyes are becoming unusally sensitive to bright sunlight, you might want to talk to your doctor about it.

While it is no doubt true that we do eat too many refined carbohydrates and processed starches, there is no solid evidence linking them to any specific eye problems—yet. That *yet* is a very important word. As we have seen, we cannot afford to be too dogmatic about the effects of nutrition on the eyes.

Although there have been many exaggerated claims made for vitamins in the past, there are credible researchers working in the field of nutrition and eye disease. One day their research just might bear fruit. Should that day come, you'll hear about it from your eye doctor.

Can Eye Exercise Help?

If you exercise your legs by running a mile, your stomach by doing 50 sit-ups, and your arms by doing 50 push-ups, how do you exercise your eyes? Do you do 50 blinks? Or try to do a push-up with your cornea?

As you can see, there is a great deal of confusion surrounding the term eye exercise. But at least it's an improvement over the other term often used for the same process—vision therapy.

Therapy, according to *Webster's,* means the treatment of a disease. If you have weak arms and you want to build up your muscles, you can go to the gym and do some weightlifting exercises. But you do not say you are performing weightlifting therapy. And it's the same with the eyes: What we're talking about is exercise, not therapy.

Strictly speaking, it's not really your eyes that get the workout. Exercise is something you do to muscles. When you talk about exercising your arm, for instance, what you mean is exercising the muscles in your arm. The rest of the arm is just there for the ride.

In the same way, you can't actually exercise your liver, your spleen, your ears, or any other organs. The eye is an organ. But you can exercise the muscles that control your eyes. Will this actually improve your vision? Let's say you have only four fingers on one hand. Whether you lost the missing finger in an accident or were born that way doesn't matter; the fact is that you are missing a finger. Will any exercise help you grow a new finger?

Of course not. But exercise will help you use your hand and

remaining fingers better. In many ways, it will help you compensate for the deleted digit. So it is with eye exercises.

Will they correct vision problems? For most eye problems, the answer, unfortunately, is no. However, there are some conditions that exercise will actually help, and we'll get to those shortly.

But first, the simple fact is that there is no scientific evidence or basis for claims that any eye exercises will cure eye conditions such as nearsightedness, farsightedness, or astigmatism. As we saw in chapter 3, these conditions are caused by the actual physical shape of the cornea and the rest of the eye. No exercise will change the shape of the eye. Can you imagine an exercise that would change the shape of your teeth?

In fact, eye exercises designed to "cure" glaucoma and cataracts are worse than useless. They can cause you to delay getting the medical or surgical care you need to prevent blindness. Exercising to "cure" glaucoma is like exercising to "cure" diabetes or lung cancer.

Studies at Johns Hopkins University, Washington University, and many other medical centers have been unable to detect any improvement of vision related such to eye exercises.

But exercises do have a place.

Strabismus, which was discussed in chapter 14, is the only common disorder that has a remote chance of being helped with eye exercises. In strabismus, one eye is turned in or out because of an imbalance in the muscles that control eye movement. Special exercises for this problem, known as orthoptic exercises, can, in certain situations, be useful when practiced under the supervision of a trained orthoptist.

Keeping Your Eyes on the Ball

Many athletes, too, use eye exercises to "improve" their vision. But what they are actually improving is their ability to track moving objects. By exercising their eye muscles, they are increasing the speed and accuracy with which those muscles will move and focus the eye.

One common tracking exercise involves taking a pin with a brightly colored head and holding it a few inches in front of your eyes. Then you move the pin back and forth, up and down, and in circles. You start slowly to make sure that both of your eyes can follow the pin as it moves. The more you do it, the easier it is to keep it in focus as it moves faster and faster.

Proponents of vision therapy believe eye exercises can be used to improve one's performance, especially in athletics. The American Optometric Association reports, for example, that Val Skinner, a member of the Ladies Professional Golfers Association (LPGA), used these techniques in 1984 to compensate for a problem judging distances. On her long approach shots to the green, she tended to see things closer and to the right of where they actually were.

Although this was a long-standing problem, she had unconsciously learned to compensate when she first learned to play golf. But as the stress and strain of being on the LPGA tour grew, the problem got worse.

Using specially designed exercises that taught her how to aim her shots to where the green really was—no matter where her eyes told her it was—helped her overcome the problem. The next season she finished in the LPGA's top ten.

It is important to realize, however, that despite success stories like this, there is still a fair amount of skepticism about eye exercises in the scientific community.

It is conceivable that tracking exercises could be helpful to people who have jobs or recreational pursuits that require them to move their eyes a great deal and to quickly change their focal points. By developing the eye muscles, eye exercises might also reduce eyestrain or eye fatigue brought on by straining weak eye muscles.

But as far as actually improving the medical condition of your eyes, or letting you do without the corrective lenses that an eye doctor has prescribed for you . . . forget it! It's been known and documented for years that eye exercises can't help in such cases.

Why, then, does the issue keep coming up? Why do the claims keep being made?

Palming and Other Panaceas

The eye-care field, like other areas of health care, has practitioners who try out new methods. Such investigation could be considered valid research. However, when methods have been fruitlessly investigated over and over, continued research is often meaningless. Even worse, when unsound claims are used to give false hope of correcting an eye problem, they may be extremely dangerous. A patient might ignore a truly helpful yet less-glamorous type of treatment, preferring to pursue an easier way to solve the problem.

Unfortunately, greed and monetary gains are the usual reasons for the practice and perpetuation of useless procedures and techniques. And one of the secrets of presenting and selling those techniques is to wrap them in mystery and mumbo jumbo.

Consider, for example, the mysterious process known as palming. Palming is nothing more than resting your eyes by covering them, and then relaxing your mind. It's a great way to dissolve tension but not one you should need to pay for.

Another eye exercise, swaying, is a rhythmic turning of the body with the eyes closed. It is also, according to some eye exercise practitioners, a "cure" for glaucoma.

Zooming is another oversold exercise. You start out by holding your thumb about 4 inches in front of your face and focusing on it. Then you look out toward the horizon as far as you can see for several seconds, and then you repeat.

Shifting is one exercise that has been called "jogging for the eyes." Without straining, you look from left to right, then up to down. Then you roll your eyes in a circle and repeat.

While palming and swaying are nice relaxation exercises, and zooming and shifting can possibly help you develop your ability to change focus quickly, they do about as much to "cure" an eye disorder or disease as they would for the common cold or a broken foot.

There are also people who claim to know eye exercises that will "cure" color blindness, refractive errors, cataracts, and macular degeneration. About the only thing that can be said for those types of eye exercise is that they are usually as expensive as they are useless.

Caring for Older Eyes

If you're like most people, you probably have a private, personal vision about what you'd like your old age—your golden years—to be like. But unless you start taking care of your eyes now (see "Nice Things to Do for Your Eyes" on page 224), that old age might be one where vision itself is limited.

Nice Things to Do for Your Eyes

- If you live in a dry climate, use a humidifier. The dryness can bother your eyes as well your sinuses.
- When you fly, sit in the nonsmoking section and do not aim the air conditioning nozzle directly at your face. Drinking plenty of nonalcoholic liquids will also help prevent your eyes, and your entire system, from getting too dry.
- If you swim in chlorinated water, put on your swim goggles before you jump in.
- If you work with a computer, take a short break every half hour or so to rest your eyes. You might also consider spending 5 minutes of your lunch with your eyes closed and your feet up.
- If you do close work, pick something far away to focus on occasionally to relax your eye muscles.
- When you're reading or doing close work, make sure you have enough light to let you see comfortably. Make sure that it's aimed at what you are looking at and that none of it is reflected back into your eyes to cause glare.
- Keep a pair of good sunglasses with you for times when the sun gets too bright or the wind blows too hard. Sunglasses can keep dirt and dust from blowing into your eyes and protect them from bright lights and ultraviolet radiation.
- If your eyes feel irritated, close them and place a warm or cool washcloth over them—whichever feels better.
- If you want to use a soothing eyedrop, try artificial tears, especially the preservative-free variety. They can be purchased in any drugstore and used as often as you wish—if the pollution index gets high, if you get dust or dirt in your eyes, or if your eyes are in the flight path of someone else's cigarette smoke.

The older you are, the more likely you are to have eye problems—serious eye problems. Statistics tell us, for example, that among every 100,000 people under the age of 18, only 60 are severely visually impaired. But among every 100,000 people aged 75 there are 13,000 cases of severe visual impairment.

Once you pass your early forties, your vision starts to lose both sharpness and elasticity. As you get older, you may need brighter light for reading, working, and driving.

Does this mean that you automatically lose vision when you get old? No. Does it mean that you are more prone to vision-threatening diseases and conditions? Yes.

Presbyopia, glaucoma, and cataracts are almost as natural as gray hair. Macular degeneration, diabetic retinopathy, and detached retinas are other conditions that hit senior citizens harder than they hit younger people.

Fortunately, the better care you take of yourself today—and that includes taking care of your eyes and visiting an eye doctor regularly—the better shape you will be in tomorrow.

If you have presbyopia, you can get reading glasses or bifocals. The latter are available as either eyeglasses or contact lenses.

Just as you should also have regular health checkups as you get older, you should have a complete eye examination every two or three years. If you have an eye problem or a family history of glaucoma or diabetes, a yearly eye exam is probably a good idea.

And if you notice any problem or change in your vision, have it checked immediately by a doctor. Don't ignore it. It's usually a lot easier to stop vision from getting worse than it is to restore once it's gone.

Spotting Alzheimer's Disease Early

An eye examination can tell the doctor a lot more about you than just how your vision is holding up.

New research shows that among the first signs of Alzheimer's disease in many people are subtle but distinct changes in color vision, depth perception, and drawing ability. All of these can be easily checked in a routine examination. If a problem is detected, treatment for Alzheimer's can start long before the disease reaches a more advanced stage.

A person with Alzheimer's disease can have 20/20 vision and still bump into things and have trouble reading. That's because the disease appears to affect the cells in the retina that are directly responsible for depth perception, motion detection, contrast sensitivity, and orientation.

WHO'S WHO IN EYE CARE

Gynecologists specialize in women, pediatricians specialize in children, obstetricians specialize in helping women deliver those children—and almost everyone else specializes in eye care. At least it seems that way at times.

Actually, there is a very limited number of men and women in a small number of clearly defined eye-care professions. But because many of the titles sound so similar—optometrist, optician, ophthalmologist, orthoptist—it can get confusing. To add to the confusion, different states have different laws about what the members of the various professions can or cannot do and what they have to do to qualify to be able to do it.

Here is a quick overview and general guide to who the various eye-care professionals are and what they do. If you have any specific questions about what these practitioners can or cannot do in your state, call one. Better yet, call several, and while you are asking them what it is that they do, also ask them what they charge. Most people shop around before they buy a new car, a house, a computer, or even a pair of shoes. You should do the same when you're in the market for eye care. Your eyes deserve it, and so do you.

Ophthalmologist

An ophthalmologist—sometimes referred to as an oculist— is a fully qualified medical doctor (M.D.) who specializes in examining and treating eyes.

Ophthalmologists diagnose and treat all diseases of the eye, including glaucoma, cataracts, strabismus, retinal detachment, vitreous disorders, infections, and inflammation.

They also prescribe medication and medical treatment, and if surgery should be required, they determine what course of action to take and perform the actual operation.

Many patients prefer to deal with ophthalmologists for routine eye examinations and prescriptions for glasses and contact lenses.

Optometrist

Although not medical doctors, doctors of optometry (O.D.s) are health-care professionals who are specially educated, clinically trained, and state licensed to examine the eyes, diagnose problems, and in some states, provide treatment.

Among the types of treatment optometrists use are prescription glasses, contact lenses, vision therapy, low-vision aids, and, in some states, pharmaceutical agents.

If you have a problem that they can't handle, optometrists know who can and will send you to them. Usually you will be referred to an ophthalmologist.

Optician

Think of an optician as a pharmacist for your eyes.

Opticians are trained to interpret a written prescription from an ophthalmologist or optometrist and then design, order, and fabricate glasses or contact lenses to fill that prescription. Also known as dispensing opticians, their job includes making sure the glasses fit properly so that the patient is seeing through them with optimal results and reasonable comfort.

Certified
Ophthalmic Technician

Certified ophthalmic technicians assist ophthalmologists by taking patient histories and performing a number of tests. They may also do contact lens fittings.

Many certified ophthalmic technicians are ophthalmic nurses who received additional training to earn certification.

Orthoptist

Orthoptists specialize in eye exercises, primarily for children with strabismus. They were much more common in the 1940s and 1950s than they are today. Most of the ones who started out then now serve as certified ophthalmic technicians.

Low-Vision Specialist

A low-vision specialist is a technician with a knowledge of highly specialized optical lenses and devices that may restore reading, writing, and driving capability to those whose vision cannot be corrected with regular eye wear.

Many of their clients have retinal problems, especially macular degeneration, which cannot be helped by other forms of treatment.

Optometric Technician

Optometric technicians assist optometrists by taking patient histories and performing some of the routine tests.

I APPENDIX B

WHAT'S WHAT IN EYE CARE

Terms associated with the anatomy, diseases, and treatment of the eye can be even more confusing than the names of the various eye specialists. The following glossary of frequently used ophthalmologic terms is reprinted with the permission of Research to Prevent Blindness, the nation's foremost voluntary organization supporting medical research in the field of blindness.

Accommodation. The ability of the eye of adjust for various distances.

Acuity, visual. Expression of acuteness of vision.

Albinism, ocular. Complete absence of pigment in the eyes.

Amblyopia. Impairment of vision with no detectable organic lesion.

Angle of anterior chamber. Junction between iris and cornea through which the aqueous flows.

Angoid streaks. Bands appearing in the retina, often associated with systemic disease.

Aphakia. Having no lens in the eye, e.g., after cataract removal.

Aqueous humor. Fluid in the anterior chamber of the eye.

Arcus senilis. A white ring around the margin of the cornea, especially in the aged.

Astigmatism. Defect in the curvature of the cornea.

Atropine. Paralyzes parasympathetic nerve action; applied locally to the eye to dilate the pupil and paralyze ciliary muscle for accommodation.

Blepharitis. Inflammation of the eyelids.

Blepharospasm. Spasm of eyelid muscles.

Blind spot. Normal defect in visual field due to position at which optic nerve enters the eye.

Canaliculus (lacrimal). Narrow tubular passage—tear duct.

Cataract. An opacity of the lens.

> **Congenital:** One that originates before birth.
>
> **Hypermature:** One in which the lens has become either solid and shrunken or soft and liquid.
>
> **Incipient:** Any cataract in its early stages, or one that has sectors of opacity with clear spaces intervening.
>
> **Mature:** One in which the lens is completely opaque and ready for operation.
>
> **Senile:** A hard opacity of the lens occurring in the aged.
>
> **Traumatic:** Cataract following an injury.

Choked disk. Swelling of the optic nerve.

Chorioretinitis. Inflammation of the choroid and retina.

Choroid. Vascular layer of the eyes; its function is to nourish the retina.

Ciliary body. Portion of vascular layer of eye whose function is secretion of aqueous humor.

Cone, retinal. Specialized visual cells in the retina, responsible for sharpness of vision and color vision.

Conjunctiva. The delicate membrane that lines the eyelids and covers the exposed surface of the eyeball.

Contact lens, corneal. Contact lens molded for the cornea only.

Contact lens, scleral. Contact lens molded to the entire globe, not containing the cornea.

Cryosurgery. Use of low temperature in surgery.

Cyclitis. Inflammation of the ciliary body.

Cycloplegia. Paralysis of the ciliary muscle.

Dacryocystitis. Inflammation of the lacrimal sac.

Detachment of retina. A condition in which the inner layers of the retina are separated from the pigmented layer.

Diathermy. Coagulation of tissue by heat such as used in retinal detachment surgery.

Diopter. A unit to designate the refractive power of a lens.

Diplopia. Double vision.

Electroretinogram. A record of the changes of potential in the retina after stimulation by light.

Endophthalmitis. Inflammation of the internal structures of the eye.

Esotropia. Deviation of the visual axis toward that of the other eye (cross-eyes).

Exophthalmos. Abnormal protrusion of the eyeball.

Exotropia. Deviation of a visual axis away from that of the other eye (walleyes).

Extraction. The surgical removal of the lens, e.g., cataract removal.

Fluorescein. A fluorescent yellowish dye used in determining the fit of contact lenses or in the detection of corneal abrasions; also may be injected intravenously to study blood vessel pathology of the eye.

Fovea. A depression or pit in the center of the macula; it is the area of clearest vision.

Glaucoma. A condition of the eye characterized by increased intraocular pressure.

> **Acute, closed- or narrow-angle:** Glaucoma caused by obstruction of the filtration angle by the base of the iris.

> **Chronic simple, open-angle:** Glaucoma in which the angle of the anterior chamber is open and free from any obstruction.

> **Congenital:** Glaucoma present at birth due to a defect in the angle of the anterior chamber.

> **Absolute:** A final, hopeless stage in which vision is completely and permanently lost.

Gonorrheal ophthalmia. A blinding eye disease of newborn infants that is acquired in the birth canal.

Herpes simplex. An acute virus disease marked by groups of watery blisters on the skin and mucous membranes; the most common cause of blindness due to corneal disease.

Intraocular pressure. The pressure of the fluid within the eye.

Iridectomy. Surgical removal of part of the iris.

Iridocyclitis. Inflammation of the iris and the ciliary body.

Iritis. Inflammation of the iris.

Keratitis. Inflammation of the cornea; usually characterized by loss of transparency and dullness.

Lacrimal. Pertaining to the tears, or to the structure conducting or secreting tears.

Lens. Lens of the eye: A transparent biconvex body situated between the posterior chamber and the vitreous through which the light rays are focused on the retina.

Lenticular. (*adj.*) Pertaining to or shaped like a lens.

Leukoma. A dense white opacity of the cornea.

Levator muscle. Muscle that raises the eyelid.

Macula. An oval area in the center of the retina devoid of blood vessels; most responsible for color vision.

Muscae volitantes. Normal small floating spots seen when looking at a bright uniform field such as the sky; attributed to minute remnants of embryonic structure in the vitreous humor.

Myopia. Nearsightedness.

Myopic degeneration. A form of nearsightedness that may lead to blindness.

Needling (of cataract). A surgical procedure in which the lens is punctured to allow the absorption of the lens substance.

Neuritis, optic. Inflammation of the optic nerve.

Neuroblastoma. Retinoblastoma.

Opacity. The condition of being opaque.

Ophthalmoscopy, direct. The observation of an upright mirrored image of the interior of the eye.

Ophthalmoscopy, indirect. The observation of an inverted image of the interior of the eye.

Optic atrophy. Degeneration of the optic nerve fibers; visual loss usually accompanies this condition.

Optic disk. The portion of the optic nerve within the eye that is formed by the meeting of all the retinal nerve fibers at the level of the retina.

Optic neuritis. Inflammation of the optic nerve.

Orbicularis. An eyelid muscle that closes the eye.

Orbit. The cavity in the skull that contains the eyeball.

Orthoptics. The teaching and training process for the elimination of strasbismus.

Pallor of disk. Paleness of the optic nerve, suggesting atrophy.

Paracentesis. Surgical puncture of a cavity for the aspiration of fluid, e.g., aspiration of aqueous humor.

Parasympathetic. (*adj.*) Pertaining to the nerve system that, in the eye, activates pupillary constriction.

Pathway, visual. The neural path of visual impulses.

Perimeter. An instrument for measuring the field of vision.

Phakoma. A small grayish white tumor in the retina.

Phoria. Any tendency of the eyes to deviate from normal.

Photophobia. Abnormal sensitivity to and discomfort from light.

Pigmented epithelium. A layer of cells in the retina containing pigment granules.

Presbyopia. Impairment of vision due to advancing years or old age.

Pterygium. A growth of the conjunctiva considered to be due to a degenerative process caused by long-continued irritation, as from exposure to wind and dust.

Pupil. The opening at the center of the iris of the eye for the transmission of light.

Reflex, pupillary. Constriction of the pupil when stimulated by light.

Refraction. The determination of the refractive errors of the eye and their correction by glasses.

Refractive errors. A defect in the eye that prevents light waves from being brought to a single focus exactly on the retina.

Retina. The innermost of the three tunics of the eyeball, surrounding the vitreous body and continuous posteriorly with the optic nerve.

Retinal hole. A space where the retina has pulled away from the underlying choroid tissue.

Retinitis pigmentosa. A hereditary degeneration and atrophy of the retina.

Retinoblastoma. A tumor arising from retinal germ cells.

Retinochoroiditis. Inflammation of the retina and the choroid.

Retinopathy. A disease of the retina due to various causes.

    Diabetic: Changes in the retina due to diabetes mellitus.

Hypertensive: A disease of the retina associated with essential or malignant hypertension.

Retinoscope. An instrument for measuring the refractive state of the eye.

Retrolental fibroplasia. A disease of the retina in which a mass of scar tissue forms in back of the lens; associated with premature birth and oxygen inhalation.

Sac, conjunctival. The potential space, lined by conjunctiva, between the eyelids and the eyeball.

Schlemm's canal. A circular channel at the junction of the sclera and cornea through which aqueous humor leaves the eye.

Sclera. The tough, white, protective coat of the eye.

Screen, tangent. A large square of black cloth, stretched on a frame and having a central mark for fixation, used to map the field of vision.

Segment, anterior. Referring to the front part of the eye.

Separation of retina. Separation of the retina from the pigmented epithelium layer.

Slit lamp. An instrument producing a slender beam of light for illuminating any reasonably transparent structure, such as the cornea.

Spectrum, visible. That portion of the entire spectrum that contains wavelengths capable of stimulating the retina.

Squint. Strabismus.

Squint, accommodative. That which is due to excessive or deficient accommodative effort.

> **Convergent:** That in which the visual axes converge (cross-eyes).

> **Divergent:** That in which the visual axes diverge (walleyes).

Stereopsis. Visual perception of depth or three-dimensional space.

Strabismus. Squint; failure of the two eyes to direct their gaze at the same object simultaneously, because of muscle imbalance.

Sty. Inflammation of one or more of the sebaceous glands of the eyelids.

Tear film. Microscopic film that constantly bathes corneas.

Tonography. The recording of changes in intraocular pressure produced by the constant application of a known weight on the globe of the eye.

Tonometer. An instrument for measuring the pressure inside the eye.

Trachoma. A chronic, contagious, viral infection of the conjunctiva and the cornea.

Ulcer, corneal. Pathological loss of substance of the surface of the cornea, due to progressive erosion and death of the tissues.

Uveitis. Inflammation of the vascular coat of the eye (choroid, ciliary body, and the iris).

Vision, central. That which is elicited by stimuli impinging directly on the macula.

Vision, distant. Vision for objects at a distance (usually 20 feet).

Vision, near. Vision for objects at a distance corresponding to normal reading distance.

Vision, peripheral. That which is elicited by stimuli falling on areas of the retina distant from the macula.

Visual acuity. Ability of the eye to perceive the shape of objects in the direct line of vision.

Visual axis. The line of gaze.

Visual cortex. Final station of visual impulses in the brain; sensory area of brain responsible for vision.

Visual field. The area of physical space visible to an eye in a given position.

Vitreous or vitreous body. Transparent, colorless mass of soft gelatinous material filling the eyeball behind the lens.

Water drinking test. Provocative test for glaucoma; the patient drinks 1 quart of water after fasting, and the intraocular pressure is measured every 15 minutes.

Xerophthalmia. Conjunctivitis with atrophy and no liquid discharge; produces a dry, lusterless condition of the eyeball.

INDEX

Page references in *italic* indicate illustrations.

Rodale Press, Inc., publishes PREVENTION, America's leading health magazine.
For information on how to order your subscription,
write to PREVENTION, Emmaus, PA 18098.